INNER HEALING

# INNER HEALING

## A SPIRITUAL PROCESS

### DAN JOSEPH

QUIET MIND PUBLISHING

Quiet Mind Publishing, LLC
PO Box 4024
Greenwich, CT 06831

(800) 758-5761 book orders (24 hrs/day)
email: info@quietmind.info

ISBN: 0-9716267-1-5
Library of Congress Control Number: 2002091739

*Inner Healing* is a book about opening to an inner experience of God's love. It is not meant to be a substitute for professional psychotherapy or other forms of counseling.

First Printing: July 2002

# CONTENTS

—

# BORDERS®

## Returns to Borders Stores:

Merchandise presented for return, including sale or marked-down items, must be accompanied by the original Borders store receipt. Returns must be completed within 30 days of purchase. The purchase price will be refunded in the medium of purchase (cash, credit card, or gift card). Items purchased by check may be returned for cash after 10 business days.

Merchandise unaccompanied by the original Borders store receipt, or presented for return beyond 30 days from date of purchase, must be carried by Borders at the time of the return. The lowest price offered for the item during the 12-month period prior to the return will be refunded via a gift card.

Opened videos, discs, and cassettes may only be exchanged for replacement copies of the original item.

Periodicals, newspapers, and out-of-print, collectible and pre-owned items may not be returned.

# Author's Note

⁂

*Inner Healing* is a book about opening to an inner experience of comfort and warmth. I believe that this sense of comfort is waiting for us, and that it simply needs an opening.

*Inner Healing* draws upon several spiritual and psychological practices, most particularly *A Course in Miracles*. For those who are not familiar with it, *A Course in Miracles* is a program of "spiritual psychotherapy" that promotes inner peace through a process of forgiveness and prayer.

In the following chapters, I will focus on a core practice that *A Course in Miracles* outlines – the practice of acknowledging our dark thoughts, and letting them be replaced by an experience of comfort and support.

At the outset, I'd like to touch on a few points about language. In this book, I use the word God in many places where *A Course in Miracles* (and other writings) would use "the Holy Spirit." I chose to do that in order to be as inclusive as possible. Please feel free to substitute for my words in whatever way feels appropriate to you.

Also, although I occasionally refer to God as "He," I don't mean to promote a view of God as masculine. Using "He" is just a language convention that is familiar to me. Again, you're welcome to reinterpret my language in a way that feels comfortable.

I will begin this book by presenting a three-step process that's inspired by *A Course in Miracles* and other writings. I'll then spend a few chapters exploring the three steps in greater detail. I'll add techniques and exercises in parts two and three of this book, and conclude with a series of notes.

I'd like to be clear that this three-step process is simply one way of opening our hearts to an experience of God's love. There are countless other approaches, all valid. However, I do find that this process is one effective way to support the experience of inner healing.

# PART ONE

—

## THE THREE-STEP PROCESS

# The Three Steps

An overview

There is a three-step process of inner healing that I have found to be very helpful in my life. Although it is a simple process, it can be powerful.

Here are the three steps:

Step 1. We honestly acknowledge some of our dark thoughts and feelings.

Step 2. We offer that darkness to God and become willing to release it.

Step 3. Having cleared a space, we now open to an inner experience of comfort and love.

That inner experience of God's love is what *A Course in Miracles* calls a "miracle." It is the goal of the three-step process.

⁂

Although those three steps are simple in theory, they are not always easy to practice. However, I find that they can produce very tangible results.

Let me offer an illustration of the three steps in order to clarify them.

I recently found myself in a conflict with a business associate of mine. He was several weeks late in signing an agreement, and I felt upset. Instead of squashing down my sense of upset, or "venting" it toward my associate, I decided to run through this three-step process.

To begin, I sat down and took note of my feelings. "I'm feeling annoyed right now," I said to myself. "I'm also feeling impatient."

I then identified some of the thoughts behind those feelings. "I think that this guy is being unresponsive and rude," I said. "I bet that he's delaying this agreement on purpose. Those are a few of my unpeaceful thoughts."

That honest acknowledgement of my thoughts and feelings completed step one. Then I moved on to step two. I brought those thoughts and feelings to God to be healed.

"God," I said, "I offer these thoughts to you. I'd like a new way of looking at this situation. I'm willing to release these old thoughts."

I spent some time handing over my dark thoughts to God, as if they were objects in my hands. As I did that, I felt a lightening in my heart.

Then I moved on to step three. "God," I said, "I'm open to a new experience of this situation. Please inspire a clearer, more loving perspective."

As I said that, I tried to hold my mind open to something new. A feeling of reassurance arose in me, and I began to see my associate in a warmer way. My sense of annoyance about the situation was gradually replaced with a greater sense of patience. As my attitude shifted, I felt comfortable giving my associate more time to respond.

That was a simple example of the three-step process. By acknowledging some of my dark thoughts and feelings (step one), becoming willing to release them to God (step two), and opening to the inflow of God's warmer thoughts (step three), my mind was comforted.

The whole process took only a minute or two. But it inspired a clearer approach to the situation. If I had ignored my sense of distress, or "taken it out" on my associate, I would have stayed in darkness. But by exchanging my unpeaceful thoughts for God's loving replacements, my state of mind was improved.

## The Love of God

The real goal of the three-step process is to open our minds (or hearts) to an experience of God's love. As I see it, it is God's love that heals us. Our job is simply to clear the way for it. In the three-step process, we identify our dark thoughts, become willing to release them, and open ourselves to an inflow of comfort.

When I began working with *A Course in Miracles*, I didn't really understand the importance of this practice. At the time, I was enchanted by spiritual ideas. I loved to gather philosophical insights. But I didn't understand that there was some active inner work to be done.

After years spent reading *A Course in Miracles* and other spiritual writings, I realized that I must be doing something wrong. I understood the ideas fairly well, but I was as unhappy as ever. It was at that point that I began to do the work that the Course describes – this active work of exchanging my dark thoughts for God's loving replacements. Suddenly, like a car stuck in the mud for years, I began to inch forward.

I'd like to be clear that I am still a beginner at this practice. I imagine that many of us are. However, I find that beginners can support each other quite well. My purpose in writing this book is to explore the three-step process, share my experiences, and offer some simple exercises for practicing.

# More Detail on the Process

❧

## A closer look at the three steps

Let me explore each of the three steps in slightly more detail. As with everything I write, I encourage you to read through these ideas and then adapt them in whatever way feels meaningful to you. I find that flexibility is essential in this type of work.

If at any point things begin to feel "theoretical," you're welcome to turn directly to part three of this book, which contains exercises for application.

Let me recap the three steps:

At step one, we acknowledge some of our dark thoughts and feelings. These may include resentments, worries, self-judgments, or other forms of upset.

At step two, we offer those dark thoughts and feelings to God to be healed.

At step three, we open ourselves to an inflow of God's love, or miracles.

Let me now take a deeper look at each of the three steps.

Step 1. We acknowledge a dark thought or feeling.

Step 2. We offer it to God to be healed.

Step 3. We open to an inflow of love, or miracles.

## Step One: We acknowledge some of our dark thoughts.

At step one, we become honest about our dark thoughts and feelings. We say, "I have a grievance against that person," or, "I'm worried about so-and-so," or whatever else is interfering with a sense of peace.

This can be a challenging step. "Bringing up" unpeaceful thoughts and feelings can be uncomfortable. It can be difficult, for example, to admit that we're feeling jealous toward someone, resentful, or afraid. But if we courageously, and with great self-acceptance, raise those thoughts and feelings to our awareness, we can exchange them for the love of God.

At step one of the three-step process, we make note about where we feel blocked – anxious, sad, angry, or whatever. We don't need to verbalize this to anyone (although we may want to involve a trusted partner in this process). Either way, our job is to become honest about our dark thoughts and feelings. This prepares us for the next two steps, in which we release those blocks to God and open to a miracle of inner healing.

I've found that people who try to "stay positive" in their lives may have difficulty with step one. Acknowledging an angry or self-attacking thought may feel like a step backward. Admitting to feeling sad or lonely may conflict with an effort to "stay upbeat." It may seem better to keep the dark thoughts hidden.

*A Course in Miracles*, however, asks us to honestly acknowledge any blocks so that we can quickly hand them over to God to be healed. At step one, we simply admit to ourselves where we feel stuck.

## Step One Avoidance Tricks

The mind can play some funny tricks to avoid acknowledging its dark thoughts. I find that sometimes when I'm upset, I search for someone to "pin" my thoughts on instead of admitting what's going on inside.

For example, I remember having a conversation with a friend of mine that went like this:

Friend: "How are you doing?"

Me: "I'm fine. But I'll tell you – this guy I know is being really annoying."

Friend: "So you're feeling upset?"

Me: "Oh, no – I feel great. It's just that this person is acting annoying."

Friend: "I see. So you're feeling annoyed."

Me: "No, I told you – I'm wonderful. I feel great. It's just that this guy is acting dumb."

In that situation, I didn't want to acknowledge my dark thoughts and feelings. I didn't want to admit that I was angry or annoyed. Instead, I wanted to see another person as the entire problem. I chose to focus on his "annoying behavior" instead of admitting that *I* was in a state of annoyance.

This kind of circle can go on for a long time. The Course (and many psychologists) call this "projection." Instead of acknowledging our own dark thoughts – for example, the fact that I felt annoyed – we focus on someone else's behavior. We try to "project" our dark thoughts by seeing them outside of us.

Step one of the three-step process reverses this cycle. It turns our focus to our own state of mind. To be sure, there are many people in the world who are acting in unkind ways. But that isn't, in my opinion, what we need to focus on. I believe that we need to focus on healing our *own* dark thoughts and feelings. At step one, we identify where we are in need of a change.

As we identify some of our dark thoughts – our grievances, worries, and so forth – we don't need to analyze them. We simply need to become aware of them. That completes step one. Once we have done that, it is essential that we quickly move on to step two.

## Step Two. We offer our dark thoughts to God, and express our willingness to release them.

Having become aware of our dark thoughts and feelings in step one, the Course asks us to immediately bring them to God to be healed.

As I see it, our dark thoughts are like splinters that stick into us and cause us pain. At step one, we admit that we're being troubled by the thought splinters – not just the outside situation. At step two, we turn to the doctor and ask him to take the splinters out. If we were to stop at simply identifying our dark thoughts (step one), we wouldn't experience much relief.

Some people pause at this point and say, "But I've tried to change my mind. I just can't stop my dark (angry, fearful) thoughts." I understand this response. When we're in a state of distress, it can be difficult to single-handedly lift ourselves out of it. However, *A Course in Miracles* doesn't ask us to do the work by ourselves. We're not asked to change our dark thoughts into inspired ones using only our own personal efforts. Rather, we're asked to turn to God with our darkness and allow Him to heal us.

There are countless ways to practice the handing-over-the-dark-thoughts process of step two. A simple approach that I often use is a short prayer:

God, here are my dark thoughts.
They are causing me pain.
I am angry at this person,
Frightened about that situation,
And I feel guilty because I see myself as a failure.
These thoughts and feelings are hurting me.
I give them to you.
Thank you for your comfort and healing.

The key at step two is the desire to have God remove our unloving thoughts, and the willingness to let the exchange happen. It is my experience that God always responds to this invitation when we say it and truly mean it.

## Imagery

I sometimes use symbolic imagery in this "releasing" process – particularly if I feel unfocused. When I do this process with one friend of mine, we bundle together our unforgiving thoughts and offer them to God like a bunch of packages.

Other times I feel the weight of my dark thoughts as if they were rocks in a backpack that I've been carrying around. I try to experience how burdensome my dark thoughts are. Then I hand that burden over to God, feeling the weight leave me.

Water can also be a helpful image. We can feel God washing away our painful thoughts like a cleansing rain. Or we can see ourselves dropping our old thoughts into a river that carries them away. We can watch them float downstream, cleansed from our minds.

There are other support methods besides imagery. I know one man who actually stands up and raises his hands during this process as he says out loud, "God, I release this to you." Including a concrete, physical movement helps him to release his painful thoughts.

I don't think that there is any one "releasing" format that's best for everyone. The key is simply to offer the thoughts to God, the Inner Healer, and let Him do His work. If imagery, prayers, or any other technique helps us, we can certainly use it. If we wish to just quietly increase our willingness to open our darkness to God, that too is wonderful.

Once we have identified a dark thought, and offered it to God to be removed, we can then move on to the final step of the three-step process.

## Step 3. We open our minds to the inflow of God's new, inspired, loving thoughts.

As I see it, God's love is like an eternally flowing river. There is no end to it, and it wishes only to flow into and through us. The experience of God's love can be temporarily blocked by our dark thoughts – our grievances toward others, our self-attacking thoughts, and so on – but the instant the blocks are removed, the river flows through our hearts once again.

Because of this, step three in the process requires the least amount of work. At step one, we become aware of an inner block. At step two, we offer that block to God to be removed. Step three is the reward step for our work. At step three, we simply open our minds to the inflow of God's love, wisdom, and comfort.

I believe that every one of us needs the experience of this comfort. The Course points out how many ways we seek for comfort outside ourselves – through worldly acquisitions, bargaining relationships, and so forth. I have spent years seeking comfort and security through those forms, and have never found it there. The Course asks us to learn that the comfort we seek is available right now; it simply needs an opening.

Step three does require some effort on our part, but the effort is directed at keeping the channel open. In step one, we found the sluice gate in the dam. We threw it open (with God's help) in step two. In step three, God's loving thoughts begin to flow back in. Our job now is to make sure that the gate stays open.

When *A Course in Miracles* refers to a "miracle," it is talking about the experience of step three. As God's inspired thoughts reach us, our minds are healed. But that isn't all. As God's love returns to us, our whole experience of the world is altered. We are filled with a sense of compassion and peace, which spills out from us into the world. The inner healing that takes place at step three truly is a miracle.

As the Course points out, the external issue that sparked our need for an inner healing may or may not seem to change. But externals will fade into the background as we're filled with an inner experience of God's love. We have found and handed over the core problem in steps one and two – the core problem being our resentments, our sense of aloneness, and so forth. We are receiving a core correction in step three – an inner, personal sense of God's care for us. That healing-at-the-core is what the Course is focused on.

At times we may identify a dark thought at step one, and ask God to remove it at step two. But then we don't immediately feel a great inflow of love, or miracles. I don't consider this to be a sign of failure. God's love may enter our awareness as a little stream at first, so that we're not overwhelmed.

Many of us have spent years generating dark thoughts and attitudes. It may take some practice before the habits we've developed are reoriented. If there's one thing that the Course has taught me, it's that persistence, gentleness, and a calm, patient approach is essential in this type of work.

## Outflow

There is an additional part of step three that could possibly be split off as a "step four." However, in the interest of keeping things simple, I'd like to include it in this step. The addition is the practice of allowing God's love to extend through us to other people.

As I wrote earlier, I look at God's love as a river. Just as a river doesn't flow into our land and stop there, so God's love doesn't terminate with us. It needs to flow through us, to others.

Because of this, I find it helpful to allow the inner miracles of step three – the new, inspired thoughts and feelings – to extend outward to other people I think about, and other things I see. As those miracles flow out, they continue to flow in.

As an example, let's say that I pause during a conflict with a friend to practice this three-step process. I identify some of my unloving thoughts (step one). I then turn to God and offer those thoughts to Him (step two). A sense of peace begins to arise in me (step three).

If I stop at that point, I will have moved in the right direction. However, if I want to truly keep the river flowing, I can actively extend my newfound peace to my friend – through thoughts, words, or actions. Even if I've only been able to let in a trickle of peace, it will grow as I let it move through me.

The flow of God's love, like the flow of a river, can be blocked in two ways. It can be blocked upstream – between us and its source – or it can be blocked downstream, between us and others. Blockages on either side will impede the flow.

At the beginning of step three, we clear the inflow. We exchange our dark thoughts for God's loving replacements. But it's also important to keep the outflow clear –

to let that love flow through us. As we let God's love extend from us to others, it continues to flow in.

During our practice of step three, we may find ourselves once again blocked by a dark thought or feeling – a grievance or a flash of fear or something. If so, we can simply return to steps one and two. We can identify the block, offer it to God, and welcome the return of His love.

In my experience, this is an ongoing practice. It isn't something that we do once, and then are done with. We will undoubtedly hit a new block as we go along, or find ourselves back in some darkness. The skill is simply to recognize this, and once again turn to God for help.

# The Practice of Step One

❧

## Raising the darkness to awareness

Let me now take a deeper look at each of the three steps, beginning with the first one.

The trickiest step might be step one – the "acknowledging the darkness" step. It can be challenging to take a look at our dark thoughts. The process requires us to shift our attention from an outside situation to our state of mind. This requires some discipline – even courage.

To illustrate this, let's imagine that I experience a "crisis" at work. My normal tendency in that type of situation is to squash down any uncomfortable thoughts and feelings, and focus exclusively on addressing the outside situation.

The problem with that approach, however, is that my state of mind will influence my whole experience of the situation. Ignoring my thoughts and feelings is like ignoring a hole in the bottom of a boat, choosing only to bail out the rising water.

The Course asks us to stop and take at least a few moments to identify how we're feeling and what we're thinking. By doing this, we can locate any holes and let them be filled.

As I mentioned before, I find that this does take some discipline. When I'm faced with a problem, a panic usually sets in, and that panic steers my attention outward, toward the apparent problem. What we're asked to do in step one is pause for a moment and turn our attention within. We're asked to stop and take an inventory of our thoughts.

Let's say that a business project that I'm working on runs into a problem. As soon as I learn the news, I anxiously pick up the phone in order to address the external situation. But then I stop and sit down for a moment.

While I'm sitting, I spend a few moments practicing step one – honestly searching my mind for any dark thoughts and feelings.

"This feels nerve-wracking," I say to myself. "I see this as a disaster. I feel terrible for letting this happen."

That type of honest inner-identification takes only a few seconds. But it is a significant step. It turns my attention from the outside form to the inside content. It sets me on the path toward healing my mind.

If I refuse to do that step, I will likely pick up the phone and begin to project all of my dark thoughts outward. I might yell at someone, or become defensive and blameful. This will, of course, only add more dark thoughts to my mind. By refusing to acknowledge my inner situation, I'm not only failing to let it be healed; I'm probably going to end up increasing my distress.

If, on the other hand, I stop and identify my unpeaceful thoughts and feelings, I can gather them together and open them to God to be healed. The process begins with an acknowledgement of the inner problem.

## Feelings as Indicators

A helpful technique I have found for step one is the practice of monitoring how I feel. If I find myself falling into a state of anxiety, sadness, or anger, I try to immediately "catch" that and take a survey of my thoughts.

For example, I recently received a phone call that was related to a project that I was working on. I handled the phone call and left to run some errands.

While driving around, however, I realized that I felt quite emotionally upset. There was no obvious reason for this, but it was a good warning. I stopped the car for a few minutes and took an inventory of my thoughts.

As I turned my attention to my state of mind, I was able to quickly uncover a series of dark thoughts. They were little things, sparked by my phone call – little worries and resentments. They were, in fact, so little that I never "caught" them in the moment. But left unchecked, they snowballed. When I realized that I felt uncomfortable, I was able to stop and do a quick inner survey. This set the stage for an inner healing.

One of the ideas that I will cover in a later chapter is the idea that our thoughts and feelings are closely related. Uncomfortable feelings can be used as "signal flares." They serve as excellent pointers to the parts of our minds in need of help.

If we become very sensitive to our feelings, we can quickly identify when we are in need of comfort. At the first sign of emotional distress, we can stop and run through the three-step process. I will discuss this dynamic more fully later.

## Observation

The process of acknowledging our thoughts and feelings can actually be viewed as something of a game. The challenge of step one is to stay aware of what's running through our minds. I sometimes imagine myself like an inventory manager, watching a series of items roll by.

My only job during step one is to note each thought and feeling as it crosses my mind, and check it off. "Ah, yes – a resentment against so-and-so person. Some fear about what's going to happen next week. A sense of failure about that thing."

The aim at this step is to become aware of our mind's contents. I find that a calm – even "relaxed" – perspective is helpful. Our job is simply to stay honest about what is going on inside.

I'd like to be clear that this observation process is different from intellectual analysis. I used to believe that I had to intellectually pick apart each of the thoughts that passed by. I believed that I had to stop the conveyor belt and figure out why each thought was present, what it meant, and so forth.

I now believe that it's enough to feel our feelings, observe our thoughts, and open them all up to God. We may, of course, want to take a deeper "look" at a particular thought or feeling. But our emphasis can be on immediately opening it to God. We don't need to sit around in a state of personal analysis.

At step one, we become aware of our inner blocks. *A Course in Miracles* doesn't ask us to deal with these blocks on our own, but it does ask us to acknowledge them where they are. A calm, honest perspective can be helpful at this stage.

## "Building a Case"

I will share that I find step one to be difficult when I've spent some time "feeding" a resentment or grievance. If I spend a few hours building a case against someone in my mind, that line of thought forms a momentum. It can be very challenging to stop and turn my attention to my part in the situation – my dark thoughts, my need for healing.

To illustrate what I mean – and this will be my last point before taking a deeper look at step two – let's say that a person tells me that he dislikes some work I've done. He tells me that I've done things in an uninteresting and uninspired way. My feelings are hurt by this, but instead of admitting that, I immediately turn my attention out-ward.

"What does that guy know," I say. "He's just a critical person. I've never heard him say anything supportive in his life. He probably never says anything kind to anyone. He..."

The more I continue along that path, the farther I get from the core problem – my painful thoughts. In fact, the process of focusing on this person's "criticalness" fills my mind with ever-increasing amounts of darkness. As each minute ticks off, it will become more challenging to turn the tide of my thoughts and ask myself what *my* part is.

Let's say that – hours later – I admit that I feel terrible. I decide to practice step one. I sit down and firmly pull my attention back to my thoughts. I ask myself what I am feeling and thinking.

"Wow," I say, "I guess I feel a bit crushed. I see myself as vulnerable to this person's opinion. I'm afraid that maybe he's right. Maybe I'm a failure at this."

As I do that, I identify the real problem – my painful thoughts. If I continue to focus on what a "bad person" my critic is, I'll completely obscure the source of my discomfort. But if I honestly identify my thoughts – dark as they are – I clarify the situation. I can then quickly take the next step, which I'll cover next.

# The Practice of Step Two

❧

## Offering the darkness to God

Part of the skill involved in this three-step process is shortening any time lag between steps one and two. Ideally, we become aware of our dark thoughts, and immediately – with no pause – turn to God for healing.

I don't believe that there needs to be any gap between these steps. As I mentioned earlier, I don't believe that we need to sit around analyzing our painful thoughts once we've identified them. Our focus can be on actively turning to God for a healing of the problem.

*A Course in Miracles* often stresses the importance of "willingness" or "openness" at this stage. We don't need to sweep away our unloving thoughts by an act of personal will. We don't need to find our way out of darkness all by ourselves. Rather, we are asked to turn to God with our burden, and give Him permission to remove it. Step two is a releasing process, not an act of enormous personal effort.

I look at the mind as similar to a train. The train – the mind – will keep chugging along its track. It is a powerful thing, and doesn't need a push from us. Our job is to flip the track switch in order to reorient the train's path. One flip will send the train in a new direction.

Our sole responsibility at step two is to shift from holding onto our dark thoughts to becoming willing to let them go. That is all. We have identified our dark thoughts at step one. Now we are bringing those thoughts to God and inviting Him to heal them.

As soon as we flip the switch to willingness-to-release, we are done with this step.

## The Art of Step Two

Of course, becoming willing to release our dark thoughts can be a challenging process. Sometimes I stay stuck at this step for years, unwilling to loosen my grasp – unwilling to flip the switch. Step two may require some artistry, as we may need to engage in the strange process of "talking" our minds into letting themselves be healed.

If I'm feeling stuck – unwilling to open my dark thoughts to God – I often find it helpful to have a little conversation with myself:

Are these dark thoughts giving me a sense of peace? No, I suppose they aren't. Are they making me feel safe? Perhaps – but this isn't a very deep sense of safety. Might there be benefit to me in trying on a new set of thoughts – a set of thoughts inspired by God?

I ask myself those types of questions until my mind becomes a bit more flexible.

I find that I sometimes need to engage in this type of reasoning for a while. When I'm locked onto my old thoughts and perspectives, I'm like a child with his hand stuck in a candy jar. I'm stuck, but I don't want to let go of the candy in my hand. I could wait until I drop the candy in exhaustion. However, that could take a very long time.

I find it kinder to reason with myself like a caring adult would:

Am I enjoying the candy in my hand? No, I'm not. I'm simply stuck. Might I be a little better off if I drop the candy? Well, I might be. Might I loosen my grasp for a second or two at a time, and see how I feel?

When I do become ready – or willing – to let God remove my dark thoughts, I find it helpful to formalize the releasing process with a prayer. This type of focus can provide a concrete boost forward.

I might say something like:

God, I have clarified my thoughts and feelings as best
    as I can.
I see myself as unfairly criticized.
I feel sad about this.
I am worried that perhaps my critic is right.
Those are my thoughts and feelings, as best as I can
    state them.
They are causing me discomfort.
I offer them to you, God.
You are the Healer.
I am willing to release them to you and let you heal
    my mind.

If I say that, and truly mean it, I am done with step
two. I have flipped the switch. I have offered my inner
blocks to God. There is nothing more that I need to do at
this stage.

One thing that I look for in doing step two is an actual
"felt sense" of releasing my dark thoughts to God. I aim
for a tangible feeling of having my heart lifted, or of having
a burden removed. This isn't merely an intellectual exercise; I'm actually relieving myself of my pain. I'm offering
it to God, and feeling the sense of freedom that brings.

We may, of course, give our dark thoughts over to
God, feel a sense of relief, and then immediately snatch

our thoughts back again. If that happens, we can simply return to step one – identifying what it is we took back – and once again offer the darkness to God. I find that there is sometimes a great deal of this back-and-forth activity.

## Imagery

As I mentioned earlier, imagery can be helpful at step two – especially if we need some structure to make the giving-over process more concrete.

I believe that the best imagery is imagery that's inspired by God in the moment. However, I sometimes fall back on some old standbys.

For example, I may incorporate the following imagery into a prayer:

God, here are my unloving thoughts.
They are like hot coals that I've been clinging to.
They are causing me pain.
God, I give you this grievance.
I give you this sense of anger.
I give you this desire for revenge.
These thoughts have burned me.
I am willing to release them.
I offer them to you.

Or:

God, I have been carrying around these chains for
    years.
I bring them everywhere I go.
I am tired, God.
I am ready to let you take these chains from me.
My sense of failure.
My belief that I am all alone.
My sense of weakness.
I give you these chains, God.
Help me to feel free.

Again, I think that it's essential to aim for a felt sense
of release – an inner experience of handing over our
burden. This can immediately lift our hearts. To say, "God,
I give you this dark thought," is just a statement. But if
we say it and truly mean it, we have accomplished our
part in the exchange.

Sometimes a simple prayer isn't enough; my mind is
too locked onto its dark thoughts. In those cases, I may
try an extended imagery session.

I may choose a few dark thoughts that are troubling
me and imagine them as weights in a backpack. I pull
them out and set them before me. I take a good look at
each one before handing it over to God. As I hand over
each one, I see – and feel – it leaving my hands. I feel the

transfer of the weight. I see my painful thoughts in God's hands. I feel myself free of them.

The practice of step two doesn't necessarily require a great deal of time, but each minute spent in this type of work reinforces our desire to hand our thoughts over. If I'm only mildly ready to release a dark thought to God, I might need to spend some time developing my readiness. I might need to take ten minutes or more on this step. On the other hand, if I'm truly willing to let a dark thought go, this step can be accomplished in a moment.

I believe that emotional honesty is very important at step two. If we're feeling scared, sad, small, or otherwise overwhelmed during this process, we don't have to hide that. We don't have to fake a sense of bravado.

Sometimes I simply say:

God, I am frightened.
It is my own fear, though.
I offer it to you.
Please help me feel peace.

A simple, honest, heartfelt prayer is, in my opinion, one of the most powerful openings. When we are in darkness, we are like lost children; we don't have to pretend otherwise. The key is simply to identify the core problem – our inner distress – and turn to God for healing, in whatever way we can.

## Ownership

Before moving on to a discussion of the final step, I'd like to address a key element in the giving-God-the-darkness process. I believe that it's essential to take ownership of our dark thoughts, to whatever degree we can. We need to see ourselves as the possessors of the dark thoughts in our minds, rather than simply being at the mercy of them.

Our dark thoughts belong to us; they are ours to keep or give away. Another person may be sparking our dark thoughts – very often, this will be the case. But it's important to take responsibility for what we're thinking and feeling. If we insist that our thoughts are not ours to hand over, but someone else's, we're trapped.

This can be very insidious. I've been stuck in certain areas for years, lost in darkness because I didn't see myself as capable of handing the darkness to God. The darkness didn't seem to be within me; it seemed to be entirely out there, in the world. I saw myself as being at the mercy of someone else's dark thoughts, with no role or power of my own.

This is a dangerous place to be. If we refuse to take ownership of our thoughts, we are like kings and queens who refuse to govern our kingdoms. Our lands will become overrun with chaos. No one else can open up our dark thoughts to God; even God can't do the work for us without our cooperation. It is essential that we do our part.

There are some people who see spiritual or psychological work as passive. I feel the opposite. Searching our minds for our dark thoughts and opening those thoughts to God is an active, disciplined process. It requires some work. We may have to practice diligently for some time.

As I alluded to earlier, one of the biggest mistakes I made when I began working with *A Course in Miracles* was avoiding this type of work. I thought that I just had to read the book – that I simply had to educate myself about psychological and spiritual theory. I thought that somehow, someday, the intellectual ideas I was learning would "kick in," and I'd find myself in a state of peace.

Unfortunately, that didn't happen. What happened was that I became increasingly miserable until I decided to take some concrete steps. Once I began to identify my dark thoughts and ask God to replace them with miracles, I began to feel a hint of relief. I am still a beginner at this process, and have a great deal of work to do. But I find that this type of work produces very tangible results.

To recap, the first step in the three-step process is honestly identifying our dark thoughts. In step two, we offer those thoughts to God and try to get an actual sense of releasing them. In step three, which I'll cover next, we open our minds to the inflow of God's love – God's healing miracles. This is the goal that we're moving toward.

# The Practice of Step Three

⁂

## Opening to the inflow of God's love

Identifying our dark thoughts and offering them to God are the housecleaning steps that lead to step three. When we have cleared an opening, we have done most of the work. We are like thirsty travelers who have found our way to a well. All that's left is to drink.

Mystics and saints have talked at length about the experience of God's love. The love of God is an earth-shattering experience; it sweeps away our old concepts of ourselves and others, and reveals everything in a new light.

*A Course in Miracles* assures us that we don't have to spend years in prayer or meditation in order to experience this love. We simply need to clear away the blocks to it –

the blocks being our own unloving thoughts. As we identify and hand over a spot of darkness to God, His love
rushes in on its own accord.

Step three is a fulfillment step. It is the moment at
which we enjoy the fruit of our labors. Step one – identifying our dark thoughts – requires some courage, and can
be an uncomfortable experience. As we "bring up" a dark
thought into awareness, we may feel some unease. Step
two is a releasing step, and it requires some energy as well.
But step three requires the least amount of work. In step
three, we simply sit back and allow ourselves to be comforted. We have opened our hearts to the healing presence
of God. Now we simply accept it.

I recently heard a woman exclaim that she felt "bathed
in God's love" during this phase of the exercise. I think
that's an excellent description of the goal in step three.

One could say that, in truth, we are constantly bathed
in God's love. But we create a wall of discomfort with our
dark thoughts, and that wall prevents us from feeling the
love. As we hand over our dark thoughts and let God's
comfort once again reach us, our minds are healed.

## Little Streams

There *is* some work to be done at step three, but it is
primarily maintenance work. Our job is to keep the channel clear. In step one, we become aware of a block in the

river. In step two, we take ownership of that block and offer it to God to be removed. The river begins to flow again in step three. Our role at this point is to enjoy it, and to make sure that no new obstructions form.

I find that continuing to monitor my feelings is a helpful technique at this stage. Do I feel uplifted? Do I feel supported, comforted, and carried along? If so, I know that things are flowing well. If I begin to feel alone, anxious, or doubtful, that's a sign of a block in the river. When that happens, I return to step one – identifying the block – and hand it over, so that the experience of God's love can return.

Of course, there are times when I practice steps one and two and only feel a very slight increase in peace during step three. The love of God doesn't come forth as a river in those times. Rather, it's like a trickle, or just a few drops of water. This is probably because there are further blocks to uncover. However, I don't see that as a problem. To a thirsty person, a trickle of water is as good as a river.

It is wonderful if we feel bathed, or enfolded, in God's care and comfort. But if we only begin to feel a slight lifting of our hearts, that is good. We can sit in that stream, despite the fact that it is small. We can refuse to wander away. We can protect that little trickle as we continue to clear away the blocks.

I'd like to reiterate that in the past, I never thought this type of work was important. I didn't realize that it required patience and cooperation on my part. I figured that there was a raging river of inspiration around somewhere, and I could keep wandering until I found it. I ignored the trickles of water. I passed by many opportunities to clear channels for God's love.

After a long time spent wandering and never finding the great river, I sat down and started to work with the streams. I was discouraged at first. There were a lot of blocks, and not a lot of water. I didn't feel bowled-over by God's love. But I did feel a tiny increase in peace as I identified my dark thoughts and asked God to help me release them. That was enough to keep me working.

Like many of us, I continue to have areas in my life that are so filled with blocks that very little light comes through. Approaching those areas is like approaching a cave. It is a dark and foreboding experience. I often balk at step one, turning back. But even one dark thought identified and released creates a glimmer of light. That glimmer brings hope, and if we remain with it and continue to clear away the blocks, it grows.

I believe that step three – the experience of God's love, or comfort – is a wonderful thing, regardless of how strong the experience is. A trickle of water in a desert can be life saving. A glimmer of hope when we are in despair is equally precious.

## Extension

As I mentioned earlier, I find that the best way to throw the gate open at step three – and keep it open wide – is to let God's love flow through us to others. As we open our minds to God's inspiration, we can extend this inspiration to the people around us. In doing this, we open an ever-wider channel.

One of the most fundamental ideas in *A Course in Miracles* is the idea that we will experience God's love to the degree that we share it. The love of God is a flowing thing. It needs to move through us.

I remember the day that I first came across this idea in the Course. Up until that time, I had been spending months by myself – months in prayer, study of spiritual ideas, and so forth. Despite my hard work, my efforts weren't producing any fruit. I felt isolated and cut-off – anything but inspired. I didn't know what was wrong. I was trying my best to access God's love, but I felt bereft.

When I finally came across the idea that I could experience God's love only as I *extended* it, I was shocked. I thought that I had to "get" it all by myself, and then begin to share what I had received. The Course taught otherwise. The receiving and giving happen at the same time, says the Course – just as the river flows into and through our land at the same time. I wasn't giving anything to anyone; consequently, I could not receive.

To be clear, when I talk about "giving God's love," I don't necessarily mean anything dramatic. We can give a kind thought or word to someone. That may be all that we're able to offer at the time, and all that the other person needs. My problem was that I was focusing exclusively on trying to get to God myself. I blocked out everyone else from my mind in the process. I believed that it was a personal, solitary journey. The Course clarified why that approach doesn't work.

These days, when I begin to feel a sense of God's comforting presence in step three, I often let my mind move to other people and things, and try to let that love embrace them. I believe that this is one of the best practices for keeping the river flowing. The love of God will comfort us as long as it's moving through us.

## The Discipline

As I mentioned earlier, there may be some maintenance work to do during step three. We may need to return to steps one and two repeatedly in order to keep the experience of God's love clear.

For example, let's say that I am feeling upset about a relationship in my life. I sit down and identify my unloving thoughts about the situation – my resentments, fears, and so forth. That completes step one. I then humbly offer those thoughts to God (step two). I begin to feel a sense of peace, which I allow to grow in my awareness, and extend to the other person (step three).

Things flow well for a minute or two; I'm feeling much better than before. But then a memory comes to mind of something the other person did last week – something that really bothered me. I immediately begin to feel angry. The channel of God's love begins to become blocked.

The skill in this practice is to acknowledge that I've once again fallen off track, and need help. Despite the fact that I just ran through steps one and two, I need to do it again. I may have fallen into an old habit of thinking, or a deeper block may have surfaced. Either way, the approach is the same. I can identify the inner block – the new dark thought or feeling – and offer it to God in exchange for His love.

One of the "skills" of step three is to stay with the sense of peace, or love, until it becomes stable. Let me illustrate this by building on the example above.

Let's say that I bring my dark thoughts to God, and offer them to Him as best as I can. As I give over my dark thoughts, I begin to feel a sense of relief. A trickle of kindness begins to flow into my mind. I let that trickle grow and expand. I begin to feel quite a bit better.

However, a minute or so into this process, a thought comes to mind. "You know," I say, "this person is still acting in an unreasonable way. I have to tell her what I really think of her behavior."

If I break away from peace at that point, and start trying to "resolve" the situation from a place of anger, I'll have unwound the whole process. I'll have once again returned to dark thoughts. Most likely, my inner mess will spill out into the situation, and I will make an outer mess as well.

The alternative is to remain with step three until the peace feels solidly in place. I may very well need to respond to the outer situation, but the challenge is to do it from a clearer, more inspired state of mind. If an attacking thought comes to mind during step three, I can identify it and offer it to God. I may need to run through this cycle many times. The challenge is to stay with the process rather than breaking back into darkness.

I find that there are many temptations to "jump ship" during step three. Staying with the trickle of peace takes discipline. It's like remaining in the eye of a storm. We may feel a temptation to bolt – to frantically fight the external situations. The trick in step three is to notice when we feel that, hand the tendency over to God, and remain with His love until it becomes stable.

## A Quick Practice

I don't mean to imply that this three-step process needs to take a lot of time. In fact, steps one, two, and three can take place very fluidly in a moment or two. Let me offer a couple of examples to illustrate.

Recently I was driving down the road and someone swerved in front of me. I felt a flash of anger. At that point, there were three choices before me: I could vent my anger at the person, squash down my anger, or quickly speed through the three-step process.

I chose to run through the process. "God," I said, "I am outraged at this other driver right now. I see him as a reckless person. I think that he deserves some of his own medicine. Those are my thoughts. They are causing me pain. I give them to you, God. I'm open to a miracle – an inner healing."

That type of process – including opening to a sense of God's support – required only a few seconds. When I felt another flash of anger, I ran through the steps again. My thoughts, and thus my actions, were elevated after this – at least, to some degree. I was able to respond to the external situation in a clearer way.

As another example, I was recently waiting on a long line at the post office. Someone walked in front of me and stood ahead of me on the line. I was stunned at this. At that point, I could have expressed my displeasure toward the person, squashed down my emotions, or tried the three-step process. I decided to run through the process.

"God," I said, "I feel insulted. I see this person as way out of line here – literally. I see myself as mistreated and not respected. Those are my dark thoughts and feelings. I give them to you. Please give me a miracle of peace. Please inspire a new perception."

As I said that, I found myself filled with a greater sense of tolerance. I mentioned to the person that I had been waiting in line, but that he was welcome to go ahead of me if he was in a rush. The person apologized, and said that he would wait. The situation was resolved in a peaceful way. The process took less than a minute.

During our practice of step three, we may receive insights on how to respond to worldly situations. We may find our perspectives on the world shifting. Or we may simply feel lifted up and carried along.

All of these are wonderful. If we let it, our experience of God's love in step three will expand. As it does, our minds are healed.

# Summary

### ⚘

## Two examples

Before moving on to part two of this book, I'd like to offer a few sample illustrations of how the three-step process might look.

As a first case, let's imagine a man who is laid off from his job. This man begins to search for a new job, but he doesn't have any success in his search. Despite his best efforts, he's unable to find a new position. As the weeks go by, he begins to feel anxious and overwhelmed.

One day, feeling unable to squeeze out another drop of effort toward his job search, the man stops and turns his attention from the outer issue – the lack of a job – to his state of mind.

He begins to acknowledge his current thoughts and feelings. "God, I feel really overwhelmed," he says. "I think that I'm facing insurmountable odds. I believe this is rather hopeless. That's what's going on inside. That's as clear as I can state things." That honest acknowledgement of his thoughts and feelings completes step one.

He then immediately brings those thoughts to God. "God," he says, "I'll probably have a better time with this job search if I'm not carrying these thoughts around. I'd prefer to be at peace. I give these thoughts to you. I give you my sense of being overwhelmed. I give you my view of this as insurmountable and hopeless. My mind is open. Please give me a clearer perspective." That giving-over process completes step two.

The man then sits for a few minutes with an open mind. As he sits, he begins to feel a sense of hope rise up within him. It's only a trickle of hope, but it feels better than what he was feeling before. The man stays with that hopeful current. He keeps his focus on it, and encourages it to grow.

After a while, the man finds the sense of hope wavering. He feels old fears beginning to resurface. Realizing that, the man identifies his specific concerns and offers them to God. "God, I have a friend who was out of work for a year. That type of proposition frightens me. But I give that concern to you. Please take it from me. I want to stay with that sense of hope."

The man goes through this cycle several more times, with various different issues. After a while, he begins to feel a good deal better. The sense of hope gradually expands into a sense of confidence. "You know," the man says, "I should give my old boss a call. I think she's been doing some freelance work lately, and she may have some leads. Funny that I didn't think of that before."

That new idea feels promising. The man picks up the phone to call his boss, but as he does so, he tries to stay with the new current of hope. He keeps an eye turned toward the inner. He makes a commitment to keep identifying and opening to God any dark thoughts that arise.

Whether or not this man finds a new position immediately, he will very likely move through the process with a greater sense of clarity and support. It's quite possible that new, creative ideas will flow into the spaces in his mind that were previously occupied by anxiety and exhaustion. He will be able to address the situation with a clearer perspective.

Let me offer another illustration. Let's imagine a woman who is experiencing some conflict with her teenage son. This woman loves her son; however, their relationship has become strained. The more she sets limits for the young man, the more he rebels against them. She is at a loss about what to do.

One night the woman's son stays out very late. The woman feels that this is unacceptable behavior, but she doesn't know how best to respond. Should she double last week's punishment? Have a long talk with him? Get professional help?

Feeling confused and upset, the woman decides to focus for a few minutes on her own state of mind. "God," she says, "I feel very upset right now. Actually, I'm quite angry at my son. I see him as terribly reckless, and I'm afraid that he's going to endanger himself. I feel ashamed that I haven't been a better parent for him – if I had, maybe he wouldn't be acting like this. God, those are my thoughts and feelings. That's what's going on inside me right now."

The woman then weighs how she feels about her current state of mind. She decides that she'd be better off addressing the situation from a clearer place. She becomes willing to open her thoughts and feelings to God.

"God," she says, "I don't know how sincere I am about this, but I'm going to try to release this to you. Please take these fearful and angry thoughts. Please give me a new view of the situation, and tell me what to do."

The woman then sits for a while, holding each one of her distressing thoughts in mind before handing it over to God. She feels a palpable sense of relief as she does this. She feels each dark thought lifted from her heart. She reaches a point where her mind is open to a new set of thoughts.

"Help me to not feel so alone," she says. And as she says that, she opens her heart to the inflow of God's love. She quickly begins to feel a sense of inner appreciation – appreciation for her own devotion to her son, and for her efforts at keeping him safe. She also begins to feel a sense of faith that – despite her son's current behavior – he has the capacity to make better choices. She begins to see a previously hidden quality of wisdom in him. She is comforted by these thoughts. They feel quite different from what she had been thinking before.

In the end, this woman may feel inspired to take any number of approaches to dealing with her son's behavior. But she will be making her decision from a greater sense of clarity and peace. By allowing her own mind to be comforted, she has prepared herself to more effectively deal with her son's growing-up process.

The key in both these examples was for the people to turn their attention – at least for a few minutes – from the outer situation to their inner state of mind. If the man had continued to focus exclusively on the job search, ignoring his anxiety and sense of exhaustion, there would have been little room for God's inspiration to enter. If the woman had focused entirely on her son's recklessness, ignoring her own need for healing, she probably would have continued to "butt heads" with him. By identifying their own dark thoughts, these people were able to open to an inner healing.

I'd like to say one more thing before moving on to the next section. Although I have presented this three-step process in a rather structured, formal way, I don't think that such structure is essential.

Some people simply turn to God with an open heart, and become willing to receive His love. Clearly, that is a complete process. Some people do not need to identify their blocks, as I've discussed in step one, and formally offer them to God, per step two. These people can, in a heartfelt instant, release their darkness and receive God's love.

There are times when I am able to do that myself. However, more often, I find benefit in running through a specific process like the one I've outlined. I encourage you to use whatever approach works best for you.

# PART TWO

## ADVANCED TECHNIQUES

# Advanced Techniques

In this section, I'd like to address some techniques that I use in conjunction with the three steps. Although I've titled this section "advanced techniques," I don't mean that these techniques are for people who are advanced at the process. Rather, these techniques are designed to give us a boost when we are stuck at a particular step.

As I mentioned at the end of the last section, I don't believe that any technique is absolutely necessary. If our minds are truly open, we will be able to naturally, fluidly exchange our dark thoughts for an experience of God's love – possibly in an instant, and without a great deal of conscious work. That is my goal: to move toward that level of openness.

However, because I often encounter resistance during the process, I occasionally need to work at one step or another. These techniques are my attempt to shed light on the steps.

As I stated earlier, you're welcome to jump ahead at any point to the exercises in part three of this book. It may be helpful to try out the actual exercises first, and then return to this section if you encounter difficulties with any particular step.

# Plumes

✺

## Helps with step one

There is one important idea from *A Course in Miracles* that I'd like to explore in this chapter. The idea is that our dark feelings don't come and go on their own. Rather, our feelings are directly influenced by our *thoughts*.

Angry thoughts, for example, will produce feelings of anger. Jealous thoughts will produce feelings of jealousy. Understanding this relationship can help with the practice of step one.

This thoughts-and-feelings idea isn't unique to the Course. It's actually the basis for many approaches in cognitive psychotherapy. Although the relationship can be readily observed, it's sometimes quite hidden.

I remember being very surprised when I first came across the idea that my thoughts and feelings were related. For years I had battled with emotional storms. I had grown used to being hit by waves of fear, doubt, and anger. These emotions seemed to rise up out of nowhere, blow through my life, and eventually pass. I figured that I just had to tolerate them.

Because of this, it was quite surprising to read that my thoughts and my emotions were related. Could it be that my thoughts had some influence over these emotional storms?

I decided to spend some time observing the relationship between how I felt and what I was thinking. As I did that, the connection became clear.

When I found myself hit with a wave of anxiety, I'd take a quick survey of my thoughts. Usually I'd uncover a series of negative thoughts that preceded the anxiety – thoughts like, "This person doesn't like me," or, "I'm terrible at this type of work."

It was no wonder that I felt bombarded with waves of painful emotions – I was bombarding my mind with waves of painful thoughts. Seeing this connection was an important step. It helped me, and continues to help me, realize the source of my emotional discomfort.

To clarify this point further, let me offer a few examples of the relationship between thoughts and emotions.

| *Thought* | generates | *Emotion* |
|---|---|---|
| The thought "That guy is so rude" | | ...will generate feelings of anger. |
| The thought "I'm really bad at this" | | ...will generate feelings of insecurity. |
| The thought "I'm all alone" | | ...will generate feelings of loneliness. |

In those examples, the feelings of anger, insecurity, and loneliness didn't arise on their own. Instead, they were influenced by specific thoughts (or perceptions). Although the feelings need to be acknowledged and released, the thoughts *also* need to be replaced. Otherwise, new feelings will build up.

## Smoke and Fire

Let me share a thoughts-and-feelings analogy that I find very helpful. Dark feelings are like clouds of smoke. Dark thoughts are the fires that give rise to the smoke.

I find that where there is smoke, there is fire – where there is a painful feeling, there is a painful thought at the source. Even one dark thought can generate a large plume of uncomfortable feelings.

As an illustration of this idea, let's say that I form a grievance against someone in my life. That one grievance can create a large amount of emotional distress. Thinking about that person may feel like stepping into a smoke-filled room. The emotional smoke plume – the feelings of anger – may be quite large. However, the fire – the actual grievance – may be relatively easy to put out.

The Course doesn't ask us to thrash around in the smoke of our emotions. Rather, it asks us to move to the fire at the center of the smoke, and let that fire be quenched. If we're willing to be extremely honest with ourselves, this can be done rather quickly.

## Examples

Let me clarify what I mean by smoke plumes and fires using a couple of simple examples.

As a first example, let's say that I experience a difficult financial event in my life. As a result of that experience, I form a belief that says: "I'm really terrible with money." If I hold onto that belief, I will feel insecure whenever I have to make financial decisions.

In that case, the fire is the thought, "I'm terrible with money." The smoke plume is the feeling of insecurity that results. Left uncorrected, that one thought can create a large plume of smoke.

Here is a simple diagram of the smoke and the fire:

Smoke Plume:
A sense of insecurity about financial decisions

Fire:
The thought: "I'm terrible with money."

As the years pass, I may invent elaborate mechanisms for avoiding my uncomfortable feelings. I may refuse to get a checking account or a credit card. Or I may latch onto someone who will make my financial decisions for me. I may end up restructuring my whole life in order to avoid the sense of insecurity.

Let's say that after years of contortions, I decide to reach through the smoke plume to the source. "God," I say, "I have this belief that I'm terrible with money. I have lots of evidence to support that belief. But that thought is causing me enormous distress. Please help me to release it. Please take it from me and give me a new, more peaceful set of thoughts about myself."

That may be enough to resolve the fire. It is at least a good beginning. Again, the key is the willingness to go to the source of the smoke – our thoughts – rather than inventing further mechanisms for avoiding the uncomfortable feelings.

It does, of course, take courage to do this, and we may encounter some smoke on the way. But our emphasis can be on quickly moving to the source – our dark thoughts, or perceptions – and immediately opening up those thoughts to God.

As another illustration, let's say that I have a falling-out with a friend of mine. I say some spiteful things to this friend, and he says some to me, and we part on that note. Whenever I think of him after that, I feel a sense of anger rising up. Therefore, I try not to think of him.

In that situation, my sense of anger is the smoke plume. The Course asks me to walk into the heart of that plume, and let God heal the source. I'm not asked to tolerate my anger. I'm asked to go to the source of the anger, and let that source be healed.

Let's say that I sit down one day and move toward the center of the smoke. "I'm really angry at this guy," I say. "I see him as an insensitive person. I believe that he never respected our friendship. Those thoughts are giving rise to this anger."

I then look for even more of the source. I become as honest as possible about my thoughts. "You know," I say, "I also believe that I've failed at my half of our friendship. I see myself as a not very good friend."

Here is the smoke and the fire in that situation:

Smoke Plume:
A sense of anger about this relationship

Fire:
The thoughts:
"My friend never respected our friendship" and
"I'm not a very good friend either."

Let's say that I gather up those thoughts and offer them to God.

"God," I say, "I see this guy as insensitive and I see myself as a bad friend. Those are my thoughts and perceptions. They are causing me a great deal of discomfort. God, I give those thoughts to you. Please give me a new view of this guy and myself."

I then feel myself handing over my thoughts to God (step two) and opening to a new view of my friend and myself (step three). As I sit with an open mind, I begin to feel a slight increase in peace. A sense of tolerance arises in me. I begin to see my friend and myself as like little children who have made forgivable mistakes.

That new view – that new thought – begins to create a new plume of fresh air. I let that plume grow. I begin to feel more peaceful about the whole situation. The feelings of anger begin to clear. After a while, I feel more benevolent and kind. I decide that I wouldn't feel so bad if I were to see this friend sometime.

Now, I may or may not have uncovered the complete root of the problem. But I have identified a few elements of the fire, and have allowed God to replace those elements with kinder thoughts. I know that I have succeeded, at least to some degree, because I feel more peaceful. There isn't quite as much smoke anymore.

The challenge in this type of process is to move to the center of the discomfort, honestly identifying our specific thoughts and perceptions, rather than avoiding the whole area. In the example above, the core problem wasn't the fight I had with my friend. The core problem was my dark thoughts and perceptions – my anger-producing thoughts about him, and my shame-producing thoughts about myself.

As long as I saw my friend as insensitive, and saw myself as a bad person as well, I was going to be surrounded by smoke. There was no way around it. My painful feelings were byproducts of my negative thoughts. They were also a good indication of where the work needed to take place.

## Core Resolution

My main point in discussing this metaphor of smoke plumes is to say that if we're having trouble exchanging our discomfort for God's peace, we may want to become as honest as possible about our underlying thoughts.

It's great to say, "God, I feel upset. Please help me to feel peace." However, it's even more powerful to say, "God, I feel insecure because I think that people don't like me, and because I believe I'm uninteresting. I give that whole package of thoughts and feelings to you."

By reaching through our sense of distress to our specific thoughts and perceptions, we become more aware of the problem. We may then have an easier time handing over the fire at its core and clearing a space for an inner healing.

The most important point I'd like to share is that God can't heal our painful feelings if we continue to generate painful thoughts. If we say, "God, help me to feel better," but continue to fill our minds with a stream of attacking thoughts, we won't experience much relief.

If, on the other hand, we become honest about our dark thoughts, and offer those thoughts to God along with our dark feelings, we have gone to the root. We have identified both sides of the coin.

I do find that where there is smoke, there is fire – when I feel sad, angry, or anxious, there are specific thoughts or perceptions underlying those feelings. Becoming honest about the whole package and offering it to God creates an open space for the inflow of miracles – the inflow of God's love and comfort.

# The Crest of the Hill

❦

## Helps with step two

Once I have identified some of my inner blocks, I try to immediately release them to God. "God," I say, "Here are my dark thoughts. I've become honest about them. I want to exchange them for a sense of your love."

Unfortunately, sometimes I get to that point and nothing happens. Although I say the words, I'm still holding tightly onto my dark thoughts. I'm not truly ready to let them go.

When I first started working with this process, I'd give up at that point. I'd say, "Well, I guess that I'm not ready to release this." I'd then walk away feeling somewhat defeated.

My attitude has changed since then. These days I try to inch forward at step two, even if my willingness to release my dark thoughts isn't very strong. I find that even a slight movement in the right direction is helpful.

There is one technique that I often use when I feel stuck. Rather than aiming for a full experience of God's love, I aim for a point at which I simply say, *"I have no idea what to think."*

Going to that point of open-mindedness is like climbing to the crest of a hill. It gets me to a place where my momentum can carry me forward.

As an illustration of this, let's say that my neighbor frequently plays loud music. Every week or two, I ask him to turn his music down. He complies for a few days. However, he soon returns to his old habits.

One night, I'm awakened late at night by a blast of music. I feel a sense of anger rising up within me. I start to have some rather violent thoughts. Before taking any rash actions, however, I decide to run through the three-step process.

"God," I say, "This first step is easy. I am really angry right now. I see this guy as insensitive and belligerent. He never seems to get the message that he needs to be quieter. I believe that he's intentionally trying to bother me. Those are my dark thoughts and feelings."

But then I get stuck. "You know," I say to myself, "I really don't *want* to take the next step. I don't want to feel any sense of kindness toward this guy. I'd rather start thinking up ways to get back at him."

It's at this point that the "crest of the hill" technique can be helpful. I'm not willing – or ready – to move into a full experience of God's love. But I can at least aim for a place of open-mindedness. I can try to clear my mind of my old, dark thoughts – even if I'm not willing to go any farther than that.

"God," I say, "I'm not ready to feel anything like love toward this guy. However, I admit that my current thoughts are causing me distress. I'm willing to say that I don't know how best to respond to this situation, or how to think about this guy. That's as much as I can do right now. But I am willing to go there."

I then try to move to a place of neutrality – a place where the slate of my mind is clear. I may not be ready to go much farther than that, but I'm at least willing to empty my mind of my old thoughts.

This, I find, is a great technique. It's like climbing to the highest point on a racing course, rather than aiming for the finish line. Once we get to the point where we honestly say, "I don't know how to look at this person (or situation)," we have done the hard part. If we don't drop back, our momentum will carry us forward from there.

Let's say that, in the situation with the noisy neighbor, I bring my violent thoughts to God. I place them in His hands, and I sit for a while in a place of open-mindedness. I'm not ready to accept a full-blown experience of God's love (or peace), but I am committed to remain free of my old thoughts.

I sit at the crest of the hill for a while. I don't feel any great sense of love, but I also don't feel overwhelmed by my anger. I feel sort of "neutral." I stay with that neutrality.

After a few minutes, a thought comes to mind. I remember that my neighbor's younger brother is visiting him. "Perhaps that's the brother who's playing the music," I think. I begin to feel a tiny bit more tolerant.

Because I'm still feeling less than peaceful, however, I work to stay at that place of neutrality. I continue to monitor my mind for unpeaceful thoughts, and release them to God when they occur. I'm still not willing to feel any kindness toward my neighbor, but I'm willing to keep my mind clear of violent thoughts.

After a few minutes, the music stops next door. I continue to work on acknowledging any resentments that arise in my mind – resentments about being awakened, resentments about the ongoing music problem, and so forth. When they come up, I turn them over to God and move back into a place of open-minded neutrality.

After a while, I begin to feel sleepy. I fall back asleep still in that neutral space. When I wake up in the morning, I feel somewhat better – a bit more patient with my neighbor. I decide to leave him a note about the music, but I'm able to do so from a place of relative calmness.

In that example, the key was for me to move into – and maintain – a space of neutrality. Reaching a place where I could say, "I don't know how to respond to this situation" was all I could do at the time. Thankfully, it was all I needed to do. From there, God could ease me forward.

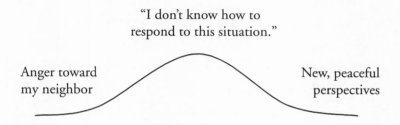

"I don't know how to respond to this situation."

Anger toward my neighbor

New, peaceful perspectives

If I had quit the process, saying, "I'm not willing to feel anything like love toward this guy," I would have stayed on the wrong side of the hill. But by moving to the crest – and refusing to drop back – I created an open space for forward movement.

## Open Mind

*A Course in Miracles* encourages us to get to the point where our minds are clear and open. The love of God will then rush in on its own – perhaps as a torrent, or perhaps as a trickle. The key is simply to create an open space. Reaching a point where our minds are clear of our old thoughts – the crest of the hill – is our primary work.

The reason that I find this idea so helpful is that, in the past, I believed that I had to take a giant leap from anger to love. On rare occasions, by an act of will, I could do that. I'd say, "OK, I'm really angry at this person right now, but I'm going to start loving him/her." I do believe that we can take that leap. However, it can be quite a challenge.

It's far easier, in my experience, to simply bring our dark thoughts to God and be willing to go to a place of open-mindedness. Then God's love can begin to flow in. Whether that flowing-in process happens quickly or slowly isn't the essential thing. We're simply asked to keep the channel clear.

If I'm having trouble moving to the crest of the hill, I often sit down and honestly measure the value of my current thoughts. Anger doesn't feel good, and it rarely inspires clear, wise action. Might I be willing to let go of my current thoughts, and admit that I don't know how best to respond to this situation? Might I at least be willing to release my pain-producing thoughts?

I sometimes need to "talk myself through" that journey to the crest of the hill. However, once I've hit a point where I can say, "Yes, it's true – I really don't know how to think about this situation," my primary work is done. An opening has been created for God to step in. As long as I refuse to slide back down the slope, I have completed my role in the process.

*A Course in Miracles* doesn't ask us to leap into perfect sainthood. It doesn't ask us to vanquish, by ourselves, all of our dark thoughts. Rather, it asks us to let God heal our minds. It asks us to gather our pain and offer it to God. Getting to the crest of the hill is all we're personally asked to do. At the crest, we come to God with an open mind and allow Him to lead us forward.

## Forgiveness

Let me add a final point about how this "crest of the hill" process relates to forgiveness. I consider *A Course in Miracles* to be, essentially, a course in forgiveness. Forgiveness is one of the central themes in the Course. However, when *A Course in Miracles* talks about forgiveness, it's not talking about a process that we do by ourselves.

In the Course's approach to forgiveness, we don't grit our teeth and say, "I'm going to force myself to feel charitable toward this person." Rather, we honestly gather up our unforgiving thoughts, release them to God, and open to the inflow of His forgiving (or loving) thoughts. It is God who accomplishes the actual healing.

When we feel that someone has hurt us, we're not asked to personally convert our sense of hurt to a sense of love. We're not asked to heal our minds using our own efforts apart from God. Rather, we're asked to move to the crest of the hill and allow God to lead us from there.

As an illustration of this, let's say that I'm in a group of people and someone makes a joke at my expense. My feelings are a little hurt. In the past, in that type of situation, I'd try to screw up a sense of toughness. I'd say, "Oh, I'm not going to let that bother me." However, I would probably hold a grudge against the person who made the joke. I might avoid him, or look for a way to "even the score." Clearly, that isn't healing.

These days, I try a different approach. To begin, I honestly admit my thoughts and feelings to myself – no matter how "petty" they may seem.

I might say to myself, "Wow, that stung a bit. That triggered a sense of insecurity in me. I'm a bit worried that I've been 'diminished' in these people's eyes by that joke. I'm feeling an impulse to 'get back' at this guy for making a joke in the first place. That's what's going through my mind right now."

Then I try to get to the crest of the hill – the place where I can exchange my current thoughts for a state of open-mindedness. I might say a prayer:

God, I bring these thoughts and reactions to you.
I have no idea how to respond to this.
I have no idea if I should laugh off this joke, or make
    a joke back, or something else completely.
I don't know how to look at this guy who made the
    joke.

I don't know how to look at myself.
I give you my old thoughts and open my mind to
    you.
Please lead me forward from here.


That is the crest of the hill. From there, God can lead me on. I don't have to "invent" a new, beneficent view of the person who told the joke. I don't have to force out a sense of kindness or tolerance toward him. All I have to do is clear a space for the inflow of God's kind, compassionate thoughts, and be willing to let them move through me.

Perhaps I choose to say nothing for a few minutes after the joke. But then I feel inspired to share that I feel a bit nervous about meeting new people. Suddenly the joke-teller's demeanor changes. He admits that he, too, feels nervous about meeting new people, and that he meant no disrespect by the joke. I thank him for his honesty. Our relationship is immediately improved.

In that example, there was a healing of my unforgiving thoughts – but the healing was done by God. My job was simply to carry my dark thoughts to the top of the hill, and offer them there to God. He moved me forward from there, and His new thoughts then spilled out into my interactions.

This is very different from the conventional view of forgiveness. In the conventional approach, we "forgive" someone all by ourselves, without any help from God. Usually this turns out to be a half-hearted attempt. We often end up simply squashing down our dark thoughts rather than letting them be healed.

In the Course's approach to forgiveness, we honestly acknowledge our pain, bring it to God, and open to His love – His miracles. Our views of ourselves and others are changed by this experience. To an outside observer, it may look as though we spun around 180 degrees through an act of will. But we know that we simply brought our pain to God and let Him relieve us of it.

I share this because when people say, "I just can't forgive this person for what he did to me," I tell them that I understand. We by ourselves can do very little. But we aren't asked to do the work by ourselves. We're simply asked to bring our sense of hurt to God – to walk to the crest of the hill.

We can lay our pain at God's feet. We can admit that we don't know what to think. We can hold our minds open to an inflow of God's comfort. And we can let that comfort flow through us to others.

As we do that, we become conduits for God's loving, forgiving thoughts. That is true forgiveness. Again, our job is simply to clear the channel; to move to the crest of the hill. Once we have reached that point, God can lead us forward from there.

# Permission Slips

❧

## Helps with step two

If I'm able to identify some of my dark thoughts in step one, but I'm unable to move to the crest of the hill – the place where I say, "my mind is open to something new" – I sometimes try an approach called "writing a permission slip."

When a young child wants to go on a school activity, she often needs a note from her parents – a permission slip. Although that permission slip is just a little piece of paper, it is a powerful thing. It opens doors to new worlds.

As a parallel, we can write "permission slips" for our minds, just as a parent would write one for a child. If we feel stuck at step two – aware of our dark thoughts, but unable (or unwilling) to release them to God – we can simply state our permission for God to release us.

For example, I might say, "God, I see myself as very mistreated right now. I am feeling angry at so-and-so person because I believe that she snubbed me. I really want to snub her back. Those are my thoughts and feelings at this moment. I feel rather locked into them, but I give you permission to remove them. That's all I can do right now. You have my permission to take them away."

That, I find, is surprisingly effective. As I wrote earlier, it's like flipping the switch on a train track. The effort involved is minimal, but it sends the train down a new route. The key is to express our permission and really mean it.

It's my experience that God needs only the slightest opening to sweep away our unloving thoughts and send in His miracles. A heartfelt statement of permission can create just this opening.

## Simple Things

At times, we may find ourselves overwhelmed by our dark thoughts and feelings. Our fear, resentment, or sense of loneliness may seem large and beyond our control. We tend to forget at these times how strong God is, and how much He wants to help us. Writing a permission slip reminds us of God's strength. It reminds us that we are the permitters of healing – not the healers ourselves.

Permission slips can be simple things. If I'm feeling anxious, a permission slip might look like this:

> God, I feel anxious.
> I feel worried that so-and-so may happen.
> I feel overwhelmed.
> However, I can do one thing – I can allow you to help me.
> I give you permission to relieve my mind of this darkness.
> You have my consent.
> I give you permission to take away my worry and the underlying thoughts behind it.
> You have my permission to comfort my mind.

If I'm feeling ashamed about a mistake I made, a permission slip might look like this:

> God, I feel terrible about what I said to that person today.
> I fear that I may have made an uncorrectable mistake.
> However, I am willing to let you heal me of these dark thoughts, and help me to make amends.
> I give you permission to take away this sense of self-condemnation.

I don't feel that I can remove these thoughts on my
    own, but I give you permission to help me.
I give you permission, God.
I give you permission to relieve me of this darkness.

We may need to maintain this sense of permission
while our minds become comfortable with the idea. We
may need to restate (or actually write out) our permission
slips several times. But if we keep our focus on our willingness to let God remove our dark thoughts, we will very
likely find our minds opening more fully to the exchange.

I do believe that we are strong enough to "hand over"
our dark thoughts to God at any moment, and be free of
them in that moment. However, when we don't feel that
sense of strength, we can simply give God permission to
do the work. I use both approaches, and find them equally
valid.

# Locking Knots

❧

## Helps with steps one and two

I have a friend who occasionally takes me rock climbing and rappelling. When my friend ties a knot in a rope, he always ties a very solid knot. However, he then ties another knot on the end – a second, small knot. He calls this second knot a "locking knot."

I once asked him about it. "You see," he said, "if the primary knot starts to slip, this locking knot will grab it and tighten. Even though it's small, it will keep the rope tied."

That struck me as a good metaphor to describe a dynamic on the three-step process. Here is what I mean:

Whenever we fill our minds with darkness, we tie our minds into a knot. Our dark thoughts are the elements of the knot, and they can be tied rather tight. It can take a good amount of work to unravel our knots.

However, that unraveling (and releasing) of our dark thoughts is profoundly complicated by a "locking knot" that we sometimes tie onto the end. The locking knot is the belief that our core problem isn't internal, but external.

Let me offer an example to illustrate what I mean. Let's imagine that a young woman saves up some money and decides to invest it in the stock market. A friend offers her a "tip" on an attractive stock, and she decides to take the plunge. She buys as much of that company's stock as she can.

A few weeks later, she finds out that the company has been involved in an accounting scandal. The stock immediately gets cut in half. The woman is horrified. She feels enraged at the company (and at her friend who recommended it), ashamed for choosing such a bad stock, and terrified about losing half of her money.

Those are the elements of the primary knot. However, instead of beginning the unraveling process – instead of admitting to herself her dark thoughts and feelings – she ties a locking knot on the end. She begins to focus entirely on the outside situation.

"What a deceitful company," she says. "I'm going to look into filing a lawsuit against them. And what a terrible friend. I'm going to tell my friend never to give me financial advice again." Her mind begins to cycle through the externals, going deeper and deeper. The more she does that, the tighter the lock becomes – and the more impossible it becomes to unravel the primary knot.

The challenge at this point is to undo the lock. The woman needs to turn her attention from the outer situation to her internal experience. Once she does that, she can let her dark thoughts be healed. But as long as she insists that the problem is exclusively external, she is going to remain stuck.

Here is an illustration of what I mean:

A Locking Knot:
"The problem is that deceitful company."

The Real Knot:
"I feel angry because I believe I have been misled. I feel guilty because I see myself as a terrible investor."

Let's say that the woman cycles through externals for weeks, going deeper and deeper into anger and misery. Then one day she sits down and says, "You know, I feel terrible. Just terrible. Maybe I should do a little inner work before I get angry at anyone else."

That tiny step unties the lock. Despite the difficulty of the external situation, she has decided to turn her attention to her inner experience.

At that point she can begin step one, which may look like this:

"I feel devastated by this. I see myself as a failure at investing. I feel ashamed about making such a poor choice. I'm angry at some other people, but I'm really angry at myself. Those are my thoughts and feelings."

She can quickly move on to step two, and offer those thoughts to God for healing. She can then move to the third step, in which she opens her mind to receive God's comforting, inspired thoughts – including guidance on any actions to take.

However, that three-step process can't begin until the woman shifts her focus to her internals – her state of mind. That shift undoes the lock.

## Inner Focus

I don't want to imply that it is easy to undo our locks and begin the releasing process. It is simple, perhaps – a simple shift in focus – but it can take a good degree of discipline. When I am confronted with a challenging situation, I often throw my focus to the externals. I thrash about for a while (sometimes a long while), flailing at the outer situation. Eventually I become tired, sit down, and begin the inner unraveling process.

Whenever we say, "My thoughts are not important here; the problem is entirely so-and-so external thing (or so-and-so other person)," we have tied a locking knot. There can be no forward movement – no real healing – until we undo the lock and acknowledge the inner problem, our dark thoughts.

There may, of course, be some important worldly actions to take in conjunction with our situation. I am not suggesting that we should ignore the worldly aspects of our lives. But if we hold our dark thoughts in place by choosing to focus exclusively on the outer situation, we're probably not going to find much relief.

One common way to tie a locking knot is to focus on someone else's mistakes, rather than on our own state of mind. This is the stuff that long-term interpersonal conflicts are made of. Instead of saying, "I feel afraid," we say, "You are doing this terrible thing and that terrible thing." We lock our own fear or anger into place by focusing exclusively on another person's darkness.

A more subtle way to form a locking knot is to ruminate on our own past mistakes. I have spent a great deal of time saying, "If only I hadn't done so-and-so, I'd be happier now." This, of course, has exactly the same effect as focusing on someone else's darkness. It locks my current dark thoughts into place. It is an avoidance mechanism – a way of avoiding an inner healing.

The alternative is to go to God with our *current* dark thoughts, and offer them to Him for healing. Instead of saying, "I should have done so-and-so differently last year," we say, "I feel ashamed (or frightened, or whatever) right now." That shift of focus undoes the lock. It allows us to begin the inner healing process – the healing of our current state of mind.

Again, I do believe that there may be some worldly actions to take in a particular situation. But ideally, we let God guide us in those activities from a place of wisdom and peace. If we made a bad decision last week, we may be guided to make amends in some way. But we can't begin that amendment process if we sit around in a state of self-abasement, fixating on how bad we are for making the mistake.

Let me add one last point about locking knots. It's important, I believe, to get to the core knot. If we try to run through the three-step process but don't find any relief, we may be fiddling about with the outer lock rather than working on the core.

For example, "I'm mad that I did a bad job at work yesterday" is a locking knot. It is a way of throwing focus away from internals. The *real* knot is, "Right now, I see myself as a failure. Right now, I'm worried that my co-workers don't like me." Those are the current dark thoughts, to be given over to God in exchange for an inner healing.

By going within, to our current thoughts and feelings, we pinpoint the area that needs to be healed.

# The Deepest Need

❧

## Helps with steps one, two and three

I find that there is a simple question that provides direction through the three-step process. The question is: "What is my deepest need right now?"

Typically, when I'm upset, I believe that I need something in the world to be different – a person's behavior, a financial situation, or something of that sort. Those may, of course, be legitimate needs – I may, for example, need money to pay my rent. However, those are not my deepest needs.

When I'm feeling stuck, I sometimes try to reach down to my deepest need. This helps to reorient me toward the process of inner healing.

For example, let's say that I'm feeling bored and alone one night. "I really need a friend to go out with tonight," I say. But none of my friends are free on this night. I sit around for an hour, feeling upset about the situation.

Then I decide to ask what my deeper needs are. What do I expect to get from a night out with a friend?

"I suppose I have a deeper need than simply going out tonight," I say. "My deeper need is a need for companionship. I want to feel connected to someone. Those are the deeper needs I'm trying to fill."

But then I try to go even deeper, to my deepest need. What does "companionship" look like to me – does it mean simply being physically present with another person? No, it's more than that. What is the deepest need I am trying to fill?

"I suppose that I want to feel a sense of love and peace," I say, "and I want to share that with other people." And that, I believe, is my deepest need. That need – the need for an experience of love, the peaceful love of God flowing through me – is what I am associating with "going out tonight."

Once I have reoriented in that way, I can begin to directly fill that need. I can remove any inner blocks to the experience of that love, and let it move through me to others. I certainly don't have to wait for a friend to call me on the phone in order to begin this process. As I create room for God's love to flow into my mind, I may feel inspired to let it flow out in any number of ways.

If I find myself in financial distress, there may be an immediate need for a certain amount of money. Beneath that, there may be a deeper need – a need for a sense of financial stability. The deepest need, however, is the need to feel safely protected in the arms of God. If I gather together some money, but don't fulfill that deepest need, I will very likely continue to find myself in a state of distress.

*A Course in Miracles* points out that our perceived needs are generally reflections of our core need to feel connected to the comfort, safety, and love of God. Without that core need fulfillment, we will remain unsatisfied. When we identify that deepest need, however, we can take active steps toward letting it be filled.

As I stated earlier, I don't mean to imply that our worldly needs should be ignored. We may need money to pay for things, and we may need friends to share our joys and concerns with. But I find that things work best when we let our deepest need be fulfilled. A moment of God's love may inspire a worldly solution, or motivate us to reach out to people in new ways. The key is to unblock things from the inside out.

Asking, "What's my deepest need in this situation?" can help us to move toward the true goal. Our deepest need – the love or wisdom of God – is everywhere, says the Course. It returns to us the instant there is an opening. It blesses us in myriad ways, and flows through us to others, blessing them. Our core needs are fulfilled in it, along with many of our surface needs. The main thing is to remember this, and to work at keeping our minds clear.

# Outflow

✾

## Helps with step three


The three-step process of opening to God's love doesn't really end with us. The process simply unblocks an inner channel, which clears the way for an outward flow.

As I mentioned earlier, there was a time in my life when I spent enormous amounts of effort on personal growth. I studied spiritual books, spent time in prayer, and so forth. However, I never seemed to get close to a real sense of peace. Looking back, one of my mistakes was that I thought the work terminated with me. I looked at spiritual work like a personal project – it was something that was going to enrich my own life. Other people didn't factor into the equation.

It was because of that orientation that I didn't get very far. I didn't understand that God's love is an extending, expanding thing – that it needs to flow through us to others.

Today, in order to stay on the right track, I try to keep my eyes on the goal of the three-step process – namely, the experience of the love of God flowing through me. The goal isn't my own separate peace or my own personal enlightenment, apart from others. Rather, the goal is to become a conduit for God's loving thoughts.

*A Course in Miracles* teaches that we will be comforted as we let God's comfort flow through us. We don't have to force this comfort, or love, out. We don't have to ramp up a personal effort to extend love, using an act of will. But we do need to clear a space for God's love to come through us. As we do that, our minds are healed.

I sometimes "backload" the three-step process by keeping my eyes on that goal. I begin by recognizing a need – a situation or a person in need of blessing. I then begin the three-step process, keeping my eyes on the goal of extending God's love to that person or situation. The process is still the same – I identify my own unloving thoughts, offer them to God, and open to the inflow of His love. However, I keep an awareness of the outflow as well.

As an illustration of this, a friend of mine recently called me on the phone. This friend was quite angry about a difficult situation she was facing. She was in need of some support. I reminded myself that if I allowed God's love to flow through me to her, *I* would be comforted in the process. Keeping that in mind, I ran through the three steps.

As I sat, listening to my friend, I turned my focus inward to my own inner blocks. I asked myself, "Where are the dark thoughts inside *me* right now?" I took a quick inventory.

"I'm feeling somewhat uncomfortable about this conversation," I admitted to myself. "I'm concerned that my friend might turn some of her anger on me. I see myself as a bit vulnerable. Those are the dark thoughts that I'd like resolved."

I then moved on to step two. "God," I said, "I'm a bit uncomfortable right now about my friend's anger. But I do want to help her – and I want to be at peace myself. I give you these blocks. I offer you my concern and my sense of vulnerability. I am willing to let you remove these uncomfortable thoughts and feelings."

I then moved on to step three, and tried to open my mind as wide as possible to the inflow of God's new, loving thoughts – God's miracles. I began to feel a greater degree of peace, mixed together with a sense of compassion toward my friend. I tried to let that peaceful compassion direct my words.

"You know," I said, "that does sound like a difficult situation you're going through."

"Yeah, it is," my friend said.

"I want to let you know that you're not alone."

She paused for a moment. "Thank you," she said.

"Is there anything I can do to help?" I asked.

And the conversation went from there. I tried to hold open the channel for God's peace, or strength, to flow through me – regardless of how "open" I was to it.

When I felt a spot of defensiveness or discomfort surface in me, I ran through the three-step process once again, releasing my dark thoughts in order to make room for God's support. I ended up doing this several times.

As the Course points out, this type of process will always help us – regardless of whether the other person recognizes our attempts to help. As we clear a space for God's comfort to flow through us, *we* are comforted.

The three-step process clears a path for this flow. Every time we identify a dark thought in our minds and release it to God, we instantly expand the experience of God's love through us. This love can then extend from us into the world, to be shared with others.

I'd like to point out that an experience of God's love can take many forms – both coming in and flowing out. God's love may come in as an experience of peace, and flow out as patience toward a family member. It may come in as a sense of safety, and flow out as kindness toward a friend. The form, I find, adapts itself to the circumstances at hand.

Focusing on the "outflow" of God's love can help to keep our minds on the right track. If we take a few moments to exchange our dark thoughts for an experience of God's love – but then, in the next minute, return to selfish or unkind habits – we will clamp the flow. Consequently, we will find ourselves back in distress.

If, on the other hand, we allow the inner miracles that we receive in step three to flow through us – to extend to others through our words, thoughts, and actions – we will keep our connection with the Source intact. A gentle word – even a smile – can keep our minds clear.

## An Example

Let me offer one last example of how the "outflow" of miracles may look.

Let's say that I'm feeling bothered by an associate at work. I've begun to dread interacting with this person. I decide to sit down and run through the three steps.

"I'm feeling upset about my interactions with this guy," I say, "but let me get clear about my specific thoughts and perceptions. What is my view of this person? How do I see him?"

I search my mind honestly, and identify several dark thoughts. "I see this person as tough to please," I say. "I see him as rather domineering. I see him as the cause of a lot of my problems. Those are some of my dark thoughts."

I then move on to step two. "God," I say, "I recognize that this isn't the highest way to look at this person. I realize that these thoughts are causing me distress. I'm willing to offer them to you. I would like to be free of them, and receive your inspired replacements – your new thoughts."

As I hand over my old thoughts, I begin to feel a trickle of peace – a hint of warmth that I hadn't felt before. I stay with that warmth, and protect it in my mind. I continue to clear away the interference to it. As I identify and release my blocks, that peaceful warmth grows. It begins to change my view of my associate.

Gradually the sense of peace expands, and I begin to feel more compassionate. "You know, I act just like he does sometimes," I say. The sting of anger that I've been feeling diminishes. Some of my associate's more enlightened qualities come to mind. I actually begin to feel a sense of appreciation for him.

Now, at that point, I've successfully run through most of the three-step process. I could conceivably stop there, glad to have received a new, more peaceful perception. I could go about my business with a more elevated state of mind.

However, the problem with stopping there is that I might inadvertently return to my old perceptions and feelings. If I want to really throw open the gate to miracles, I can focus on extending those new, loving thoughts.

For example, I may think of a few ways to share my appreciative thoughts with my associate. I may call him on the phone and extend my newfound sense of warmth to him.

I may spend some time thinking of other people in my life, and extend my sense of peace to them as well. I may simply ask God, during step three, to show me how to bless people more fully.

The point is that if I open my mind to the outflow of God's love through me – regardless of how "clear" the channel is – the flow will continue. It will very likely increase.

If, on the other hand, I enjoy a few minutes of peace and then return to my old thought patterns, I will feel like a desert traveler who has momentarily stopped by an oasis. I will look fondly back on those few minutes, but they will be like a memory.

I believe that any type of inner healing – whether it takes place in a therapist's office, in a spiritual center, or wherever – simply sets the stage for a new inner lifestyle. We will never be satisfied journeying from oasis to oasis. We need to let the water flow throughout our daily lives.

Allowing the miracles of step three to extend to other people helps to keep this river flowing. It is, I find, one of the best ways to keep the channel clear.

# PART THREE

—

## EXERCISES

# Exercises

I enjoy discussing the process of exchanging our dark thoughts for miracles. Exploring the theory behind the three steps can certainly be helpful. However, I find that the real benefit comes from actually doing the practice.

In this section of the book, I'll present a series of exercises that relate to the three-step process. As with everything I write, I encourage you to work with these exercises in whatever way is personally meaningful. If you feel that a variation of a particular exercise would be more appropriate to your situation, please feel free to use your own variation. And, of course, you're welcome to simply read through these exercises if you'd like.

In the following section, I will be making a more precise distinction between thoughts and feelings. In the earlier parts of this book, I described step one as "identifying our dark thoughts and feelings." In these exercises, I'll begin with a specific feeling, and use it as a "pointer" to identify the thoughts in need of healing.

As I mentioned earlier, our feelings can be excellent indicators of our thoughts. If we can acknowledge a distressing emotion at its earliest stage – when it's merely a hint of discomfort – we can save ourselves a great deal of trouble down the road.

As a summary, here is the general format of the exercises that I will present:

Step One: "When I think about _____, I feel _____ because I think/see/believe _____."

Step Two: "God, I am willing to release those thoughts and feelings to you."

Step Three: "God, I am open to an experience of your love, guidance, and comfort."

It is a simple format, but I find that it is quite effective.

# First Exercise

❧

## Self-perception

When I work directly with people on the three-step process, I often suggest that we write out our thoughts and feelings in step one. Writing, I find, is an excellent "focusing" tool. It helps to clarify exactly what is running through our minds.

In the following exercises, I will leave room in step one for you to write out your thoughts. You don't, of course, need to write out anything. But I find that writing can provide some helpful structure. Often I'm not aware of my specific thoughts until I put them on paper.

I will include an italicized example in each exercise to illustrate a sample response.

## Introduction

To begin this exercise, please choose some area of your life that's troubling you. It could be a relationship, a work-related situation, or anything else. If you wish, you can describe the issue below.

*(ex. My wife is bothering me about cleaning up my stuff around the house. I'm getting a little tired of it.)*

## Step One

In order to zero-in on the thoughts in need of healing, let's first take a look at our feelings. As I mentioned, uncomfortable feelings can serve as excellent pointers to the underlying thoughts.

When you think about this issue, how do you *feel*? I invite you to list out your specific feelings below.

*(ex. I feel frustrated, and a bit guilty. I also feel a sense of dread about getting into further arguments.)*

Having listed out some of our feelings, we're halfway through step one. Now let's take a look at the thoughts that are giving rise to those feelings. I believe that it's important to be very honest with ourselves at this point. We don't want to "censor" our thoughts. We're honestly bringing this darkness into our awareness so we can offer it to God to be healed.

Here is one way to bridge from the feelings to the underlying thoughts: "I feel this way because *I see myself as* _____."

I invite you to complete that sentence.

*(ex. I feel this way because I see myself as unfairly criticized. I see myself as unappreciated. I see myself as trapped by all this criticism.)*

That completes step one. We have successfully identified some of the thoughts and perceptions that need to be replaced. In this example, the person's dark thoughts were: "I see myself as unfairly criticized," "I see myself as unappreciated," and "I see myself as trapped."

Of course, those might not look like thoughts or perceptions – they might look like objective descriptions of the situation. But it's important to realize that these are just perceptions (or thoughts), and that God can inspire another perception – a perception that leads to feelings of comfort and peace.

## Step Two

Let's immediately move on to step two. Let's gather up the perceptions and thoughts that we wrote out in step one (along with their resultant emotions) and offer them to God to be healed.

As I mentioned earlier, I like to use a short prayer in this process. You are welcome to use whatever techniques are helpful to you – prayers, imagery, physical movements, or anything else that supports the releasing process. I often choose a spiritual figure who represents God's love to me, and ask him to help me release these thoughts. I support you in using whatever approach is helpful.

For the sake of this example, I will include a short prayer below.

God, I see myself as unfairly criticized.

I see myself as trapped.

I see myself as unappreciated.

However, I admit that these are my own perceptions.

I am willing to release them to you and receive
    something new.
I give you these thoughts and perceptions.
I ask you for peace, God.
I release these unpeaceful thoughts to you.
I release them to you.

At this point, I usually spend some time feeling myself actually handing over the thoughts and perceptions to God. Our goal at this point – the goal of step two – is to release the old thoughts and move into a place of open-mindedness. Regardless of how much time that takes, we can try to reach that "crest of the hill."

If you find it difficult to move into a place of open-mindedness, you may want to say:

God, I have no idea what to think about this
    situation.
I give you my thoughts.
My mind is open.
I do not know what to think.

That clears the mind for an inner healing.

When you feel a space opening in your mind for an inflow of new thoughts, perceptions, and feelings, you can move on to step three. Even a tiny opening is enough.

## Step Three

During step three, our goal is to become open to a personal experience of God's love for us. Steps one and two were designed to clear a space for this experience.

I often need to spend a few minutes at step three, seeking this inner experience of comfort and love. As I seek for it, I continue to monitor my mind for dark thoughts, and hand them over to God as they come up.

Again, it may be helpful to say a short prayer:

God, I am open to your help.
Please fill me with a sense of comfort.
I want to feel your love and support.
My heart is open to you.

Our goal at this step is to allow God's love to enter our awareness. That experience will transform our perceptions and guide our responses to the original issue. We simply need to make room for it to enter.

If dark thoughts and feelings arise during this process (and it's common for them to do so), we can again say a short prayer:

God, I don't want this dark thought.
I want to clear away the blocks to your comfort.
I give this dark thought to you.

We may need to tend to the newfound sense of comfort like a gardener would tend to little seedlings. We may need to spend most of our time clearing away the weeds of our old thoughts. But the work is worth it.

If you do begin to experience a sense of comfort or love during step three (no matter how strong it feels) you may want to give it permission to flow through you to others. You can allow it to enfold whatever or whoever comes to mind – including people connected with the original issue. As we let the love of God flow into and through us, we create an ever-wider channel for it. In the process, our minds are healed.

If you *aren't* able to feel a sense of comfort right away, you may need to "search around" in your mind a bit. This may take some practice. There is a current of peace, or warmth, somewhere in our minds, although it may be buried under layers of dark thoughts. If we search for it – and continue to release any interfering thoughts – we will clear a space for it to grow.

Once we begin to get in touch with a sense of God's love, we can let that new current of thought alter our perceptions and inspire our actions. This makes the whole process very practical. We're not just seeking a temporary oasis of peace; we're actually seeking a new way to perceive and respond to our issue. We're seeking a new inner path to follow.

## A Note on Step Three

I'd like to add a personal observation about step three. I have found that the inflow of miracles may take place sometime *after* I've completed this exercise. The full impact of step three can appear in unusual forms.

As an example, one day not too long ago I was feeling anxious about a financial concern. I ran through this three-step process in a few minutes, during a trip to a coffee shop.

"God," I said, "I'm feeling anxious because I see myself as threatened by this financial issue. I see myself in danger of some serious consequences. But I give those thoughts and feelings to you. Please give me a sense of peace."

As I finished with that process, I felt only a slight increase in peace. It wasn't much, but I decided that I would stay with it. Perhaps, I hoped, it would grow.

About ten minutes later, a man sitting across from me launched into a conversation with a third patron. We were sitting in a triangle, and I believe that the other two people had just met for the first time.

"My friend," said the man to the other patron. "I'm on a spiritual path. I have everything I need."

He said this somewhat out of the blue, and the other patron seemed surprised by the comment. "Yeah?" he said.

"I have no worries about money," said the man. "No financial concerns."

"Really?" said the other patron. "Then how do you pay your bills?"

"God provides," said the man. "I've never missed a bill yet."

"You never worry about money?"

"You just have to have faith," said the man. "I do, and things work great. I am a happy man."

At this point, I started chuckling at the obvious relevance of these comments to my situation. The other patron turned to me and asked me what I thought about the conversation.

I said to him, "I appreciate this man's attitudes. I also relate to your questions. I'm enjoying your conversation very much."

They seemed satisfied with this, and returned to their talk. After a few minutes, the man sitting across from me stood up, shook the hand of the other patron and my own, and went on his way. I was left with a model for a new attitude, and my anxieties were replaced with a sense of humor.

The interesting thing about this story is that the most dramatic inflow of God's support came to me through another person, a few minutes after I tried to open my mind to it. The full impact of step three came in an unexpected form.

I share this because I believe that it's important to keep our minds open to "inflows" of God's love in a variety of different forms. If we run through the three-step process and only feel a slight increase in peace, we can stay with that peace. Broader inflows may come to us as we go along.

# Second Exercise

✧

## Perception of others

Let me offer a parallel exercise to the earlier one. In this second exercise, instead of choosing a situation in our lives that's causing us distress, we'll choose a person whom we don't feel very loving toward.

As *A Course in Miracles* points out, we can only feel God's love to the degree that we're willing to share it with others. As we let our views of other people become healed, we open an ever-wider channel to God's love within us.

## Introduction

To begin, please choose a person whom you don't feel a great deal of appreciation toward. It could be someone you love who is currently bothering you, someone you strongly dislike, or someone whom you feel just slightly negative toward.

If you wish, you can write his or her name below.

*(ex. My supervisor Dorothy.)*

## Step One

As before, let's identify our specific feelings when we think about this person. This step calls for a great deal of honesty. It may be difficult to acknowledge some of our dark emotions – particularly if this person is a friend or family member. However, our negative feelings will point us in the direction of the thoughts that need to be healed.

Let's complete the following sentence: "When I think about this person, I feel _____."

*(ex. When I think about Dorothy I feel angry and some-what sad. I also feel defensive.)*

Let's now take an honest look at our perceptions of this person. Using our feelings as a lead-in, let's complete the following sentence:

"When I think about this person, I feel this way because *I see him/her as* _____."

*(ex. When I think about Dorothy, I feel angry, sad and defensive because I see her as a really insensitive person. I see her as someone who is in her own world – someone who never thinks about other people's feelings.)*

The final part of the above sentence represents the thoughts and perceptions in need of healing. Our current view of (or thoughts about) this person leads to our current uncomfortable feelings. God's new, inspired view of this same person will lead to feelings of compassion and peace.

Having written out our feelings and thoughts, we have completed step one. We can now move immediately on to step two.

## Step Two

It may be helpful to begin by taking full responsibility for our current thoughts about this person. I like to say a brief prayer:

> God, I take ownership of my thoughts about this
> person.
> These thoughts are mine, to keep or give away.
> I choose to give them away.
> I want to be free of my old view.
> I want to receive something new.

Then let's spend some time actually feeling ourselves offering our old view to God, to be removed. If you find it helpful to use imagery or any other supports in this process, I encourage you to do so.

Here is one form of imagery that I occasionally use:

> God, I have been seeing this person through a cracked
> set of eyeglasses.
> The cracks are my dark thoughts, and they are
> distorting my vision.
> I can't see this person clearly.
> My old thoughts are distorting my view.
> God, I'm taking off these cracked eyeglasses and
> handing them to you.

Here they are – I give them to you.
I ask you for a clearer vision of this person.

As we sit at step two, offering God our old perceptions of this person, we may want to occasionally say:

God, I don't know how to look at this person.
I just don't know.
I give you my old thoughts and perceptions.
My mind is open to something new.

When we can say that and really mean it – really feel it – we have completed step two. If it takes a bit of "handing over" time before you feel your mind becoming open, that's normal. I find that I sometimes need to engage in this offering-the-old-perception-to-God process for five, ten, or fifteen minutes before I begin to feel my mind open.

## Step Three

When you do feel that an opening has been created, we can move on to step three – the true goal.
We can say:

God, I have cleared a space in my mind.
Please give me a new view of this person.

How do you see him/her?
I don't want to use my old way of seeing anymore.
I ask for your replacement.
Please show me this person as you see him/her.

Then let's hold our minds open to the inflow of a new view. We may begin to feel a trickle of compassion enter our minds, or just a slight increase in peace. Or we may begin to receive insights into the person's behavior – insights that will inspire a greater sense of understanding in us. We may begin to sense a hint of beauty in this person that we hadn't seen before. The inflow of God's new vision can take any number of forms.

The Course points out that our view of this person will spill over into our view of ourselves. As we let our dark thoughts and feelings be replaced by miracles – God's loving thoughts – our minds are healed. Our outer relationship with this person may or may not begin to show immediate improvement. However, we will receive an inner healing in this process.

Again, the inflow of God's new vision may come over days or weeks. At times I have engaged in this process, and have felt only a slight increase in peace. However, the next time I interacted with the person in question, there was a different "tone" to my responses. Doing the three-step process set the stage for an evolving new perception of the relationship.

If we do receive a sense of compassion, tolerance, peace, or love during our practice of step three, we may want to "throw the gate open" to that love by consciously allowing it to extend to the person in question, as well as others.

We can, for example, "say" to this person as we think about him/her:

I bless you with the love of God.
You deserve it, as do I.

We can ask God to bring to mind other people who are in need of blessing, and say the same to them. That proactive "extension" of God's love will help to keep it flowing into and through us.

## Examples

In order to more fully illustrate the process of this exercise, let me offer a few examples of how it may look.

Let's say, as a first case, that a person is having an argument with her husband. She decides to run through this exercise.

She begins by identifying her specific feelings about the situation. "When I think about this conflict with my husband," she says, "I feel somewhat resentful. I also feel worried."

She then identifies the specific perceptions (or thoughts) that are generating those feelings.

"I feel resentful because I see my husband as stubborn and closed-minded. I see him as totally off the wall about this issue."

She runs through the flip side of the equation, and becomes honest about her self-perception as well.

She says, "I see myself as trapped. I see myself as powerless to resolve this situation. That's what's causing my sense of worry." That honest identification of her thoughts and feelings completes step one.

She then gathers up those various perceptions and brings them to God.

"God," she says, "I see my husband as stubborn and closed-minded. I see myself as trapped and powerless. God, I take responsibility for those perceptions. I know that you can inspire a whole new view of my husband and myself."

She spends some time "looking" at each one of those perceptions, and hands each one over to God. She actually feels her heart lifted as she does this. She begins to feel an open space being created in her mind for a new set of thoughts to enter.

After a few minutes spent handing over her old perceptions to God, and feeling them leave her, she says another prayer:

"God," she says, "please fill my heart with a sense of love and strength. Help me to see my husband and myself through your vision. God, I want to be at peace, and I want to respond to this situation from a place of peace and clarity. I am open to a miracle of healing."

The woman then holds her mind open as wide as she can, inviting a new set of inner experiences to enter. After a few minutes, she begins to feel a little more peaceful. Her mind wavers between the old feelings and this new peace, but as the old thoughts arise in her mind, she hands them over to God and returns to a state of open-mindedness.

As the minutes go by, some comforting thoughts come to mind. She realizes, for example, that she and her husband have always been able to resolve these types of arguments in a peaceful and mutually supportive way. That realization gives her hope. She also begins to feel stronger in her commitment to finding a solution to the conflict. Her feelings of vulnerability diminish, and she feels more inspired to find a resolution.

As the woman feels a sense of peace stabilizing, several thoughts come to mind to share with her husband – potential solutions to the conflict. She decides to call him on the phone and share them with him.

In that example, the woman's husband may or may not react favorably to her phone call. But by engaging in this type of practice, the woman has let her own mind be comforted. She has accepted an inner healing. This will undoubtedly assist her in her efforts to find a resolution to the relationship conflict.

Let me offer another example. Let's imagine a student who dislikes going to school. This student has never felt very close to his friends, and doesn't feel as though he "fits in" at school. He decides to run through this exercise.

"When I think about going to school," he says, "I feel stressed and upset." However, that doesn't feel like the deepest level of his emotions. He tries to become even more precise about his feelings.

"When I think about school," he says, "I feel angry at people and a little lonely." That feels like a more honest assessment of his feelings. He then goes deeper, and looks at the thoughts and perceptions behind those feelings.

"When I think about going to school," he says, "I feel angry and lonely because I see myself as left out from the crowd. I see myself as unable to fit in."

He also acknowledges his perceptions of other people. "I see the other kids as dumb," he says. "I see them as self-absorbed and uninterested in me or anyone else."

He then immediately brings those honestly-identified perceptions to God. He says, "God, I could use some help with this. I'll try to open my mind to a new view of myself and the other kids. I'll trade my old views for something new."

He then imagines himself handing over his old views to God, and letting them be taken away. His mind becomes a bit more open.

"Give me something new," he says, and as he says that he opens his mind to a new, more peaceful view of the situation.

As this young man sits, holding his mind open to a new view of himself and his fellow students, a couple of realizations come to mind. He remembers that, last week, another student invited him to lunch, but that he refused. "Maybe that kid could use a friend," he says. "I don't know why I said no to him."

He also begins to realize that the "bravado" of the popular kids at school is really just a cover for insecurity. "It's all an act," he says. For the first time, he really sees it. His anger toward the other students changes to something more compassionate. "They're probably feeling bad, too," he thinks.

As he sits, keeping his mind open to a new view of himself and his fellow students, he begins to feel a sense of appreciation for his own talents. "I'm a pretty nice guy when I'm in a good mood," he says, "and I like to help people. Maybe I can try harder to reach out to other kids who could use some help."

After a few minutes, he feels a bit better. He decides to try to keep these new thoughts in mind at school the next day – especially the realization that the bravado of the "in" crowd is a mask for insecurity, and that he him-self can reach out to other kids who are feeling alone. He feels complete with the process.

In that example, there may or may not be a magical transformation of the student's experience at school the next day. But at least an opening has been made for some-thing new.

By identifying his painful feelings and underlying thoughts – and becoming willing to exchange them for something more inspired – this person has taken a step toward peace of mind. He may need to run through this process hundreds of times before a new, more peace-pro-ducing set of thoughts becomes stable. But every step is helpful.

# Troubleshooting

※

Before offering another exercise, I'd like to outline some potential "trouble spots" on this three-step process. Knowing about these common stumbling points may help to clear up some difficulties.

I'd like to be clear that the following conversations are hypothetical. I wouldn't disclose someone's actual struggles with this process. However, the following conversations represent similar ones I have had.

## Troubleshooting Step One: Feelings

In working with people on these exercises, I find that one of the most trouble-prone areas is the identifying-the-emotions step. I sometimes have a conversation that goes like this (and I have had these same troubles myself):

Me: "To begin, please choose a situation in your life that's causing you discomfort."

Person: "Sure – I just got socked with a huge tax bill. I'll use that."

Me: "OK. Now, when you think about your tax bill, how do you feel?"

Person: "I feel that the government is ripping me off."

At that point, I would stop the exercise and try to help the person more closely identify his or her feelings. "The government is ripping me off" isn't really a feeling. It's a perception. The actual feeling is probably anger, or a mix of anger and insecurity, or resentment, or something of that sort.

When I find it difficult to identify my own emotions during step one, I often run through a list of feelings and "try on" each one. For example, I say, "Do I feel sad about this? No, not sad really. Angry? No, more like insecure. Insecure and a little anxious." That type of process helps me to become more honest about what I'm actually feeling.

I sometimes run through a similar process with other people. It might look like this:

Me: "When you say that you feel the government is ripping you off, do you mean that you feel angry?"

Person: "Darn right I feel angry."

Me: "OK, anything else? Maybe a little frightened?"

Person: "Not frightened. But maybe a little nervous."

That is a much clearer identification of the emotions. The person can now say, "I feel angry and a little nervous," and move on to the next step.

Other people have trouble identifying their dark feelings because they're well-versed in psychological or spiritual theory, and understand that negative emotions aren't necessarily "rational." However, that intellectual understanding can be a block to actually acknowledging the feelings. Here is how that type of problem may arise:

Me: "You mentioned that your job is troubling you. When you think about your job, how do you feel?"

Person: "Well, I know I should trust God with this."

Me: "That's definitely the goal. But let's take a look at what you're actually feeling."

Person: "But I understand that there's really no reason to feel bad about this. I know that bad feelings don't accomplish anything."

Me: "OK, but let's begin at the beginning. How do you feel right now?"

Person: "I know that I should just have faith."

And so on. The intellectual understanding – true as it may be – is a block to the acknowledgement of the actual feelings. In a conversation like that, I might share how *I* would feel in a similar situation, and use that as an opening for the other person to agree or disagree. For example:

Me: "If I were to go through a situation like the one you're describing, I imagine that I might feel a little angry, and perhaps sad."

Person: "Really?"

Me: "Sure. Now, you might feel something completely different. I'd be interested in hearing what your feelings are."

That sometimes helps the person to feel more comfortable identifying his or her feelings. I also try to be clear that identifying feelings is simply part of step one. It sets the stage for an inner healing. Identifying feelings is not the healing itself, but it can be a very helpful preparatory step.

## Troubleshooting Step One: Perceptions

One of the trickiest parts of step one is identifying perceptions *as* perceptions. For example, I may have a conversation like this. (And again, I sometimes have the same difficulties as this person.)

Me: "You were able to identify your specific feelings; that's great. Now let's go on to the next part of step one. You feel angry because you see your boss as...?"

Person: "I feel angry because my boss is rude."

Me: "I think that it's important to say, 'because I *see* my boss as rude.'"

Person: "But he is."

Me: "He may be acting in certain ways. But it's important to get clear about our own thoughts, or perceptions of the situation."

Person: "Believe me, if you knew him, you'd understand what I mean. That guy is rude."

In this situation, the person is having some difficulty identifying her perception of her boss *as* a perception. It's true that the boss may be acting in insensitive or unkind ways. But in order to clear a space for God's comfort to enter her mind, this person needs to gather together her current thoughts and offer them to God. Focusing only on the boss's behavior won't create this opening.

In this case, I might say:

Me: "I understand that your boss isn't showing much kindness toward you."

Person: "Yeah, that's right."

Me: "We can't work on him, though."

Person: "Unfortunately, no."

Me: "OK, why don't we focus on clearing out our *own* dark thoughts. Do you have any dark thoughts about your boss?"

Person: "I guess I do. He really triggers a lot of negativity in me."

Me: "OK, why don't you list out some of those negative thoughts. Then we'll offer them up to God, and ask for a replacement."

The key in step one is always to become clear about our own feelings and thoughts. Even if someone else is "triggering" those feelings and thoughts (and this will often be the case), we'll only find peace by working on our side of the equation. Acknowledging our specific thoughts clears the way for steps two and three.

## Troubleshooting Steps Two and Three

Steps two and three have their own unique challenges. When I help people with the three-step process, I sometimes lead a "guided meditation" for steps two and three. We might spend a few minutes on each step. Talking through these steps helps to clear up a lot of problems.

When I'm doing the process by myself, however, I sometimes find my mind wandering during steps two and three. Short prayers and imagery are great; I often use them. However, when I need some additional help, I use a technique inspired by *A Course in Miracles* and many other spiritual and psychological practices: the technique of a "focusing prayer."

A "focusing prayer" is a short idea or statement that we repeat to ourselves, over and over, as a way of focusing the mind. The goal is to use the words to go beyond the words, into an actual experience of peace and release. Let me offer a few illustrations of what I mean.

Let's say that I'm able to identify some of my dark thoughts and feelings in step one. However, as I offer them to God, I find my mind wandering. At that point I may begin to repeat a phrase as a centering point for my intention. For example:

God, I release these thoughts to you.
I release them to you.
I release them to you.
I release them to you.

I may need to repeat that phrase dozens or hundreds of times in order to keep my mind focused and on-track. The goal isn't simply to repeat the phrase; the goal is to use the phrase to go into an actual *experience* of release. It is a way of focusing the mind.

Because step two is a clearing step, I might use a statement of open-mindedness as follows:

God, my mind is open.
I don't know what to think.
I don't know what to think.
I don't know what to think.

Again, the repetition of that phrase is simply a way of strengthening my intention to open my mind. Like a set of train tracks, it supplies some structure for the journey.

A step three focusing prayer may look like this:

God, your love enfolds me.
Your love enfolds me.
Your love enfolds me.
Your love enfolds me.

The phrase serves as a reminder of a truth. It is a way of directing my mind toward the actual experience of that love. It is a way of focusing my attention on my goal.

Another step three focusing prayer may be:

I seek your peace, God.
I seek your peace.
I seek your peace.
I seek your peace.

If, during the repetition of that phrase, I begin to actually *feel* a sense of peace, I will probably let the phrase drop away. If my mind wanders, I may take up the repetition again.

The use of a focusing prayer is just one method of retaining focus during steps two and three. However, I find it to be an enormously powerful tool. Incidentally, the workbook of *A Course in Miracles* makes extensive use of this type of practice.

# Additional Exercises

❧

## Beliefs and Thoughts

I have found that some people prefer a slightly different variation of an exercise. Because of that, I'd like to present a couple more "flavors" of the earlier exercise in an attempt to broaden the approach.

In the first exercise, we looked at our self-perceptions. Saying, "I see myself as _____" accomplished this. In the second exercise, we looked at our perceptions of (or thoughts about) other people.

In this third exercise, we'll take a look at the *beliefs* that we hold about a situation, rather than our specific perceptions.

143

## Introduction

To begin, please choose some issue in your life that is troubling you. If you'd like, you can describe the issue below.

*(ex. I want to quit my job and do something more fulfilling. I really don't like my current job.)*

## Step One

Next, let's identify our specific feelings. As before, I invite you to complete the sentence, "When I think about this issue, I feel _____."

*(ex. When I think about this issue, I feel a bit frightened. A little confused, too.)*

Previously, at this point, we would identify the self-perceptions and perceptions of others that led to these feelings. In this variation of the exercise, we'll take a slightly different approach. Let's use the following sentence as a bridge to our thoughts: "I feel this way because *I believe that* _____ ."

*(ex. I feel frightened and confused because I believe that I might make a bad mistake. I believe that jobs are hard to come by, and you better stick with what you have. I believe that I might not be qualified to do anything but this job.)*

The variation here is that instead of identifying our perceptions, we're identifying our underlying beliefs. Perceptions and beliefs are so entwined that this variation might produce identical results to the previous one. However, some people are more easily able to identify their beliefs rather than specific perceptions.

## Step Two

Once we have listed out our limiting beliefs – some of which may seem "silly" or "irrelevant" and others of which may feel "true" – let's be sure to offer them all to God. We'll trust Him to sort them out for us.

I like to say a prayer at this point. I may say:

God, I am concerned about this issue with my job.
I feel frightened and confused about it.
I feel that way because I believe that jobs are hard to
     come by, and I might make a terrible mistake.
I also believe that I might not be qualified to do
     anything else.
But God, I am willing to loosen my grip on those
     beliefs.
I don't know what to believe about this job situation.
I give those old beliefs to you, God.
My mind is open.

That type of prayer can help us to clear out a space in
our minds for God's inspired thoughts to enter – new,
loving thoughts that will foster new beliefs and perceptions.

## Step Three

As we do feel an opening being created, let's immediately move on to the final step. We may wish to say:

God, my mind is open to you.
Please inspire a new set of beliefs.

I am willing to hold my mind open to an inflow of
   your love.
Help me to know that I am protected.
Inspire me.
Transform my beliefs, God.
I am open to you.

As always, our goal in steps two and three is to clear
the slate of our personal thoughts (in this case, our beliefs)
and create room for the inflow of God's loving, wise, comforting thoughts. By admitting that we don't know what
to think, and opening ourselves to a new set of thoughts
inspired by God's love, we make room for the miracle of
an inner healing.

The person in the example above may find her whole
belief system altered by this exercise. She may experience
a shift in attitude that allows her to more fully appreciate
her current job. Or she may begin to feel more empow-
ered to seek a new, more fulfilling job. God's wisdom and
inspiration can come in any number of forms.

## Thoughts

Here is a final variation of the same exercise. Instead
of identifying our specific perceptions or beliefs, we'll
simply take a broad inventory of our thoughts.

## Introduction

To begin, please choose a situation that is troubling you.

*(ex. That person's cell phone is ringing very loudly, and it's distracting me.)*

## Step One

Next, let's identify our specific feelings, as unpeaceful as they may be. Let's use our typical format of, "When I think about this issue, I feel _____."

*(ex. When I think about this issue, I feel angry and a bit vengeful. Like I want to make this guy feel bad for setting his phone ringer so loud in a public place.)*

Now let's simply take an inventory of whatever thoughts are crossing our minds in regard to this issue.

I invite you to state whatever you're thinking about the situation:

*(ex. This guy is a total boor. I mean, give me a break. Doesn't he realize how rude it is to let his phone ring like that in a public place? He probably likes the attention.)*

The key at this point is to realize that our feelings are coming from these thoughts, rather than from the external situation itself. God can clear away these anger-producing thoughts and replace them with peace-producing thoughts, once we allow that exchange to take place.

## Step Two

Once we have taken an inventory of our thoughts, let's immediately offer them to God to be released. Let's say:

God, I have honestly identified my thoughts.
I realize that they are producing discomfort in me.

I give these thoughts to you, God.
I don't want them anymore.
I want to create a space for a new set of thoughts.
God, I give these thoughts to you.

Then let's hold our minds open to an inner healing –
an inflow of God's inspired, loving thoughts. Just as our
old thoughts produced distress, God's new thoughts will
produce peace.

## Step Three

Let's say this, as we move into step three:

God, my mind is open.
I don't know what to think about this situation.
I really don't know.
But I'm willing to receive your thoughts on the
    matter.
Please fill my mind with your peaceful thoughts.
I am open to something new.

Then let's hold our minds open to an inflow of wiser,
more peaceful, more inspired thoughts. As we do this, we
receive an inner healing – regardless of what happens on
the outside.

# Ongoing Practice

❧

The exercises that I presented have focused on specific situations in our lives that are causing distress. I'd like to conclude by broadening the scope of this practice.

The real goal of the three-step process is to clear out our old perceptions of everything, and let the love of God rush in to take their place. If we can get to the "crest of the hill" with everything we see, we can open our minds to God's peace-producing vision of those things. Ultimately, this can be a fluid, ongoing practice.

Let me share how this process may look. I may be sitting in my office one day. I decide to spend a minute looking around myself and running through this exercise with everything in my field of vision.

"When I look at that computer," I say, "I feel some annoyance because I see it as outdated. God, I give that perception to you. I don't know how to look at this computer. Please inspire a new view of the computer that brings me joy."

I spend a few seconds offering my old perception to God, and holding my mind open to a new, peace-producing perception of the computer. I actually begin to feel uplifted by the computer. Then I move on to something else.

"When I look at that desk," I say, "I feel some frustration because I see it as falling apart. But I also feel some appreciation because I see it as a good companion over the years. God, I bring that mix of perceptions to you. I don't know how to look at this desk. I give you all my old thoughts about it. Please inspire a new view."

I spend some time opening my mind to the beauty in the desk, and then move on to the next thing.

"When I look at these phone messages, I feel overwhelmed because I see myself as trapped by a lot of external demands. God, I give you that perception. Please inspire a new view of these phone messages."

And so on. When I'm sitting in traffic, or waiting at the post office, I sometimes run through this type of exercise. The goal is to open my mind to God's vision of all these things – thus clearing out my old, limited thoughts and views.

## People

For a more challenging version of this ongoing practice, we can use people.

For example, I might be waiting on line in a store. As I overhear various conversations, I acknowledge my thoughts and offer them to God in exchange for something more loving.

The process might look like this:

"When I see that man, I feel angry because I see him as a mean-spirited person. But God, I don't know how to look at that man. Please take my old perception of him, and inspire a new, loving view. How do you see him?"

"God, when I see that woman, I feel a little nervous because she seems rather intimidating. But God, I am not seeing that woman as she really is. I give you my perception of her. Please show me this woman as you see her."

"God, when I see that couple I feel some impatience because I see them as crowding my space with their arguing. God, I give you that view. Please inspire a more compassionate set of thoughts toward this couple."

Underlying this practice is the idea that our personal perceptions of people are always limited, to some degree. As we allow God to inspire a new perception – a perception based on His love – our views are elevated and our minds are healed.

## Conclusion

My goal in this book has been to share a simple practice that supports the experience of inner healing. In the three-step process, we identify and release some of our dark thoughts, which clears an opening for the inflow of God's loving thoughts.

I'd like to state once again that there is nothing special about this process. It is just one method of opening our minds, or hearts, to God's love. If you feel that a variation of the three-step process – or a different process altogether – would help you to more fully experience God's love, I support you in using whatever works for you.

There are, of course, some people who go through their days feeling a perpetual connection to the love of God. These people do not need a specific practice; they are receiving an inner healing all day.

For those of us who are not yet at that stage, I find that the three-step process can help. In the following section, I will provide some references to this process from *A Course in Miracles* and other writings, and explore a few points in greater detail.

Thank you for reading, and I wish you the peace of God.

# Part Four

NOTES

# Notes

❧

I'd like to begin this section by sharing a conversation that I have had, in one form or another, with various people. It goes like this:

Person: "I'm trying to stay positive, but it's really hard."

Me: "I understand. You know, this three-step process isn't about trying to stay positive."

Person: "It's not?"

Me: "No. This process is about admitting how frightened or angry we feel, and then bringing those thoughts to God for an inner healing."

Person: "You mean that it's OK to feel afraid?"

Me: "I think that we have to be honest with ourselves."

At this point, many people have expressed relief. Some people had been bottling up dark feelings for a long time, in an attempt to "be positive" or "have faith." To hear that they didn't need to hide things anymore was a significant relief.

I share this because inner healing, in my opinion, begins with an honest acknowledgement of our inner blocks. In this three-step process, we first acknowledge and lift up our dark thoughts to God, and then let them be swept away by His love.

Let me recap the three steps:

In step one, we acknowledge some of our dark thoughts and feelings.

In step two, we offer them to God to be healed.

In step three, we hold our minds open to an inflow of God's comforting love.

I'll now provide some references for each of these three steps. This is a very incomplete list, but if you'd like to read further, the following may be of interest.

## Step One References

There are many sections in *A Course in Miracles* that encourage us to "seek out" our dark thoughts.

This strikes many people as a strange practice – after all, why would we want to *seek* for our resentment or fear? The reason, says the Course, is that our dark thoughts can't be released if we bury or hide them away. By honestly acknowledging them, we can quickly let them be replaced.

For those who would like to explore the Course's take on "acknowledging the darkness," one of the most descriptive (and powerful) sections is the Text, Chapter 13, Section 3. In addition, many Workbook lessons include a "searching for the darkness" step – including, for example, Lessons 5, 21, and 34.

Becoming aware of unpeaceful or limiting thoughts is also a central practice in many forms of cognitive psychotherapy. For those who would like to explore this field in more detail, two of the largest schools of thought are Cognitive Therapy (or Cognitive Behavior Therapy), based largely on the contributions of Dr. Aaron Beck; and Rational Emotive Behavior Therapy, founded by Dr. Albert Ellis.

The work of Richard Carlson also strikes me as belonging in this field. His books, including *You Can Be Happy No Matter What* and *Shortcuts through Therapy*, offer some excellent approaches to working with currently-held thoughts and perceptions.

## Step Two References

Step one of the three-step process is similar to many psychotherapeutic techniques. In step one, we identify some of the specific thoughts that are giving rise to our emotional discomfort.

However, step two begins to approach a practice of spiritual healing. Instead of trying to straighten out our thinking all by ourselves, we bring our darkness to God and invite Him to heal it. We may, of course, want to use prayers, affirmations, or other supports in this process. But the focus is on opening our darkness to God and receiving His love.

One of the clearest instructions to "give over" our dark thoughts is in the Text of *A Course in Miracles*, Chapter 7, Section 8, Paragraph 5. This section asks us to immediately hand over our darkness to God (or, more precisely, the Holy Spirit) once we have uncovered it. It is His job to heal it; our job is to give it to Him. Another reference to "giving over" our dark thoughts is in the Course's Workbook Lesson 151, Paragraph 14.

My incorporation of imagery in this step two process is based on techniques that the Course uses. For example, Workbook Lesson 69 uses the image of moving through clouds into an experience of God's love (the clouds symbolizing our dark thoughts, or grievances).

I'd like to be clear that I don't believe it's the imagery itself that heals anyone. It is the love of God that heals. The imagery is simply a supportive technique for opening our minds (or hearts) to that love.

## Step Three References

Step three, in which we open to a sense of God's comfort, is what the Course means by "prayer." The Course describes true prayer as an opening of the heart, rather than a request for things. The *Song of Prayer* pamphlet, an official "supplement" to *A Course in Miracles*, covers this theme quite well – particularly in Part 1, Section 1 of the pamphlet.

The Course also provides many references to what it calls a "holy instant" – basically, a time in which our minds become quiet and open. God's loving thoughts can then rush into that open space. This is what happens in step three. Chapter 15 of the Text of *A Course in Miracles* contains many descriptions of the holy instant.

The mystic and spiritual healer Joel Goldsmith wrote extensively about this type of experience. One of his major teachings was that we shouldn't try to "invent" an inner healing all by ourselves; rather, we should allow God (or God's love) to enter our awareness and do the healing. Some of Joel's wonderful books are *The Art of Spiritual Healing* and *Living the Infinite Way*.

The "extending" idea that we can only receive God's love to the degree that we share it is mentioned throughout the Course. Workbook Lesson 108 is one clear example of this teaching. Chapter 9 of the Text, Section 6, Paragraph 2 also gives a nice mention.

As a final note, a parallel to the overall three-step process can be found in Workbook Lesson 23, Paragraph 5.

That is a small sample of references to the three steps. Let me now give some additional commentary on specific ideas from the book.

### From "The Three Steps," p. 13

"If I had ignored my sense of distress, or 'taken it out' on my associate, I would have stayed in darkness. But by exchanging my unpeaceful thoughts for God's loving replacements, my state of mind was improved."

I'd like to provide a follow-up on the conflict with my business associate.

Although I did feel an increase in peace after running through the three-step process, I found myself back in distress about the situation later that day. I ended up re-running though the process ten or fifteen times over the following few days. Each practice helped a bit.

Later that week, I found myself feeling comfortable about the situation – despite the fact that the business issues were still unresolved.

Soon thereafter, I learned that there had been a mix-up in the mail. It turned out that my associate had sent me exactly what I requested, but I hadn't known it. The whole "conflict" – based on my perception of him as rude and unresponsive – was in my mind.

I'd like to be clear that I needed to run through the three-step process several times in order to reach a sense of peace. In that case, one practice wasn't enough. I share this because I don't want to foster the idea that the three-step process is a magic bullet. It's simply a structure for reorienting the mind – a process that may require patience and persistence on our part.

From "More Detail on the Process," p. 18
"The Course (and many psychologists) call this 'projection.' Instead of acknowledging our own dark thoughts...we focus on someone else's behavior."

*A Course in Miracles* seems to put most psychological defenses into two main camps: projection and denial. Let me briefly touch on both of these. I'd like to be clear that these descriptions are extreme simplifications of the concepts, and that I may be using the words in a different way than some psychologists would.

In projection, a person "sees" his or her darkness in someone else. For example, a person who is projecting his dark thoughts might say, "I'm a very cheerful person, but everyone around me is always angry." This person doesn't want to admit that he himself is angry, or feeling hurt or frightened or whatever. Therefore, he "sees" his dark thoughts and emotions exclusively in other people.

Denial, as I am using the word, is a bit different. A person who is in denial may simply say, "I'm doing fine. Nothing is bothering me." People who are in denial often feel "nothing" – neither emotional warmth nor emotional discomfort. They may feel "in a fog."

To be clear, I believe that most of us are using both projection and denial all the time. If a person were to suddenly stop using both, she'd probably be engulfed in an intense sense of discomfort stemming from her dark thoughts, and, simultaneously, an overwhelming sense of God's love. It could be a rather traumatic experience.

I believe that a wise approach is to gently, gradually lay down these defenses one small piece at a time. For example, we can acknowledge one or two of our uncomfortable feelings. This reduces our use of denial. Then we can "take a look" at some of the thoughts that are giving rise to those feelings. This reduces our use of projection, as it brings our attention from the outside situation to our state of mind.

Of course, those are only step one elements. Once we have uncovered (or become honest about) some of our dark feelings or thoughts, it's essential to turn to God for an inner healing. Mere awareness of our darkness doesn't, in my opinion, accomplish the healing. It is the experience of God's love that heals and comforts our minds.

From "The Practice of Step One," p. 29

"A helpful technique I have found for step one is the practice of monitoring how I feel. If I find myself falling into a state of anxiety, sadness, or anger, I try to immediately 'catch' that and take a survey of my thoughts."

I believe that monitoring our feelings is one of the most helpful habits we can form.

There are many wonderful teachings on developing emotional awareness. One approach comes from the work of Marshall Rosenberg, author of *Nonviolent Communication: A Language of Compassion.*

I have a friend who is a teacher of Mr. Rosenberg's Nonviolent Communication. When I first met this friend, I was struck by his emotional depth. We had several exchanges that went like this:

Me: "Hi there – how are you doing?"

Friend (pauses to ascertain): "A little sad. But also hopeful and even a bit enthusiastic."

I was stunned by that level of emotional richness. My friend was never just "fine." He was perhaps joyful and hopeful, or anxious and angry, or some other mix. But he was always willing to "check in" on his specific emotional state.

I find this type of emotional awareness to be a powerful practice. As I mentioned elsewhere in this book, our emotions can serve as excellent indicators of our thoughts.

If we can recognize when we're feeling a hint of sadness or anxiety, we can immediately stop and identify the thoughts that are leading to those emotions. We can then turn to God for an inner healing. The work begins with the emotional hint.

Let me add one last point on emotions. I remember having a conversation with a friend when I started working with *A Course in Miracles*. At the time, I was in a state of great inner distress. I had reached what felt like a breaking point.

"I suppose that I have a low tolerance for emotional pain," I said. "I just can't deal with this anymore."

"No," said my friend, "I think that you have too *high* a tolerance for emotional pain. That's why you've been struggling for so long."

I didn't understand what she meant at the time, but now I can see it. We are not asked to build a tolerance to emotional discomfort. Rather, we're asked to become *intolerant* to it. We're asked to become so sensitive that we turn to God at the first hint of distress, and ask Him for healing. Squashing down our emotional pain won't make it go away. Turning to God with it will make it go away.

*A Course in Miracles* has several references to the practice of monitoring our feelings. See, for example, the Manual for Teachers, Question 18, Paragraph 4. In addition, Chapter 23 of the Text, Section 2, Paragraph 22 has a nice reference to emotional awareness.

From "The Practice of Step Two," p. 42

"We need to see ourselves as the possessors of the dark thoughts in our minds, rather than simply being at the mercy of them."

I've met a few people who don't like the image of "handing over" their dark thoughts to God. They prefer other approaches, and I certainly support them in using whatever works for them. However, let me share why I like the "handing over" image.

When we gather together and hand over some of the dark thoughts in our minds, we are implicitly taking ownership of them. To "hand over" something implies that we have it in our possession, and can do whatever we wish with it. It is, for me, a good framing metaphor for the process.

By contrast, if I were to say, "God, my darkness is so big. Please rescue me from it," I would be perceiving my dark thoughts as more powerful than I am. They may seem that way, of course. But to pick up handfuls of that darkness and offer those handfuls to God to be removed is to take ownership of the dark thoughts. For me, it puts things in a more empowering perspective.

Having said that, I'd like to add that the Course sometimes uses a metaphor of "going through" the darkness instead of "handing it over." Workbook Lesson 69, which

I referenced earlier, uses the image of moving through clouds of our dark thoughts to the light of God.

I support people in using whatever approach works best for them. I think that the most important thing is simply to open our darkness to the light of God, regardless of how we envision that.

### From "The Practice of Step Three," p. 47

"It is wonderful if we feel bathed, or enfolded in God's care and comfort. But if we only begin to feel a slight lifting of our hearts, that is good. We can sit in that stream, despite the fact that it is small."

The image of "sitting in the stream" came to me one day as I was struggling with an issue.

I felt that I could only clear away about one percent of my dark thoughts regarding this issue. But then the idea came to me that I could sit in that tiny space as I continued to do the clearing work.

The image of "surfing" came to mind – standing on a little surfboard amidst the giant waves. It might take work to stay in the tiny space of peace, keeping an awareness of God's love amidst the turmoil, but at least I could try.

I share this because I don't believe that we need to dive into our dark emotional waves. We *do* need to be aware of our dark feelings and thoughts, but we can try to do so from a space of peace and God-connection – even if it's only a tiny space. We may very well fall off the little surfboard. But if that happens, we can return to it and stand up again.

From "Plumes," p. 65

"The idea is that our dark feelings don't come and go on their own. Rather, our feelings are directly influenced by our *thoughts*."

I want to give a reference to this idea from *A Course in Miracles*, as the Course doesn't contain an enormous amount of commentary on this subject. The reference is the Manual for Teachers, Question 17, Paragraph 4. This section describes the relationship between thoughts (or, more precisely, interpretations) and emotions.

To provide some additional commentary on this thoughts-and-emotions relationship, let me offer the example of several lottery winners.

Let's say that four people win a prize in a lottery. In response to this event, these people experience four different emotions. One person is elated; another is suspicious. A third person is frightened, and a fourth guilty.

If you were to look into these people's minds, you would probably find the following (or similar) thoughts:

Person One: "What an amazing thing! This is just the break I've been waiting for!" Those thoughts will produce feelings of elation.

Person Two: "I don't believe it. This is probably a big hoax." That will produce a sense of suspicion.

Person Three: "Oh, no. My whole life is going to change. Everyone is going to be asking me for things." Those thoughts will produce feelings of fear, or anxiety.

Person Four: "I don't deserve this. Who am I to win the lottery." Those thoughts will produce (or reinforce) a sense of guilt.

The point is that our thoughts (or interpretations, or beliefs) exert a strong influence over our emotions. Different interpretations of the same event will produce different feelings.

I'd like to again state that identifying our thoughts and feelings is only step one in the three-step process. The Course asks us to immediately bring the distressing thoughts and feelings to God in exchange for a direct experience of comfort.

### From "Aiming for the Crest," p. 76

"I aim for a point at which I simply say, *'I have no idea what to think.'* Going to that point of open-mindedness is like climbing to the crest of a hill."

This "crest of the hill" technique – in which we move into a state of open-mindedness – is, in my experience, a powerful one. It is directly inspired by many sections in *A Course in Miracles*, including the Text, Chapter 14, Section 11. Paragraph 12 of this section gives a particularly strong message that open-mindedness is the prerequisite for learning.

At times, the Course reminds me of the philosopher Socrates, who said in the *Apology*, "I know that I have no wisdom, small or great." This wasn't, in my opinion, false modesty on the part of Socrates. Rather, I believe that this attitude allowed Socrates to clear the slate of his own little thoughts, and open to the higher wisdom for which he became famous. The Course advocates a similar approach.

### From "The Deepest Need," p. 97
"*A Course in Miracles* points out that our perceived needs are generally reflections of our core need to feel connected to the comfort, safety, and love of God."

This idea again ties into the concept of projection. If we feel a sense of spiritual disconnection, we'll often begin to search for outside "reasons" to blame. The Course encourages us to realize that both the source of our emotional distress and the resolution to that distress are within us. The source is our dark thoughts. The solution is an experience of God's love.

Workbook Lessons 79 and 80 cover these ideas in some detail. Lesson 90, which is a review of Lessons 79 and 80, adds some additional commentary.

I will share that I find it very challenging to keep this in mind. When I'm feeling anxious, my mind often begins to project or "externalize" that anxiety. Instead of saying, "I feel anxious," I say, "that business situation is really dangerous," or "that person is a threat to me."

The challenge is to bring the focus back within. My emotional distress is coming from my dark thoughts. A sense of peace will come from an experience of God's love. There may, of course, be some external issues to respond to – perhaps some challenging externals – but an inner healing won't come from simply rearranging the externals. The inner healing will come from exchanging my dark thoughts for God's loving replacements.

### From "First Exercise," p. 118

"I have found that the inflow of miracles may take place sometime *after* I've completed this exercise. The full impact of step three can appear in unusual forms."

This, I feel, is a very important point. There have been times that I've gone through the three-step process and only experienced the tiniest increase in peace. But then, hours later, an inspired thought came to mind that helped me. The key was to stay with the process, rather than deciding that "it didn't work."

I have found that the actual inflow of inspired, loving thoughts may come through the words of another person, through some writing in a book, through a comment on the radio, or as an idea that simply "pops" to mind. This inflow may happen during the formal practice of step three, or hours or days later.

The key is to at least stay at the crest of the hill – to keep a sense of open-mindedness and receptivity to God's loving thoughts. If we remain with a sense of receptivity, miracles can flow in. But if we break away in frustration, the door (at least temporarily) swings shut.

I do find that it takes discipline to keep an open, receptive mind. But that is the work in step three. If we can maintain that receptivity, we will stay open to God's comforting thoughts.

### From "Second Exercise," p. 121

"As we let our views of other people become healed, we open an ever-wider channel to God's love within us."

I'd like to briefly comment on this idea, as it is so central to *A Course in Miracles*.

One could, I believe, extract the following logic from the Course:

1. We will be happy to the degree that we feel God's love flowing through us.
2. Our unloving thoughts are the only blocks to this love.

3. Therefore, we will be happy to the degree that we release our unloving thoughts.

Using that as a foundation, it becomes clear why *A Course in Miracles* focuses so extensively on forgiveness. Forgiveness unblocks the inner channel to everything we seek – the comfort, wisdom, and love of God.

Of course, as I mentioned earlier, *A Course in Miracles* has a unique approach to forgiveness. In the Course's approach, we don't "forgive" a "bad person" through an act of personal will. Rather, we acknowledge our unforgiving thoughts (toward others and ourselves), and turn to God for an inner healing.

It is God's love that heals our minds and accomplishes the shift of attitude. Our job is simply to bring our dark thoughts to Him, and open our hearts to His loving replacements.

From "Troubleshooting," p. 138

"When I need some additional help, I use a technique inspired by *A Course in Miracles* and many other spiritual and psychological practices: the technique of a 'focusing prayer.'"

I am using the phrase "focusing prayer" to describe the practice of repeating a word or idea in order to focus our minds and enter into an experience of God's love.

*A Course in Miracles* encourages the use of focusing thoughts (or prayers, or affirmations). For example, many of the Course's workbook lessons encourage us to slowly repeat the lesson title. As I mentioned earlier, however, these words are meant as a lead-in to a direct *experience*. The goal isn't simply to repeat an idea like "God is Love." Rather, the goal is to repeat that idea as an entrance to an experience of that truth.

In my own practice, I usually let the centering phrase fade away once I begin to experience a sense of God's presence. I may repeat it as needed if my mind begins to wander. But once I am feeling a sense of God's love, the words become superfluous.

I believe that the Course supports this approach. For reference, see the Workbook, Part 1, Review V, Paragraph 12.

My use of "focusing prayer" is inspired by *A Course in Miracles* and also by the description of "centering prayer" articulated by the Trappist monk Thomas Keating. In addition to Keating's work, there are many other prayer and meditation practices that make use of centering thoughts.

## About the Author

Dan Joseph works extensively with *A Course in Miracles*. He is the author of *Inspired by Miracles*, a book that explores three themes in the Course. For the past ten years, he has served as a consultant in various fields. Dan can be reached via his website at www.DanJoseph.info.

*published by*
Quiet Mind Publishing, LLC
info@quietmind.info
(800) 758-5761